Make Key Stage 3 Matter in Eng

The KS3 curriculum plays a critical part in giving students the best possible start to their secondary education and preventing the need for intervention later on. This timely book provides detailed guidance on how to develop a robust, multifaceted, inclusive and challenging KS3 curriculum in English that provides a secure and progressive link between KS2 and KS4.

Featuring examples of curriculum models and audits of current practice, chapters cover key topics such as:

- developing the planning cycle;
- transitioning between primary and secondary English;
- assessment in KS3 English;
- creating a model that supports and challenges students of all levels;
- LAC and SPAG: divisive or cohesive abbreviations;
- speaking and listening in the KS3 English curriculum;
- using multimodal texts;
- examples of how meaningful homework can successfully embed itself in a KS3 English curriculum model.

Make Key Stage 3 Matter in English will be an invaluable resource for KS3 English coordinators, teachers and all those involved in the planning and delivery of the KS3 English curriculum.

Liz Hillier is an English teacher and KS3 Advisor at Claydon High School, UK. She has also been a Key Practitioner for secondary English in Suffolk and runs personal development courses for teachers on curriculum design.

Make Key Stage 3 Matter in English

Liz Hillier

Routledge
Taylor & Francis Group

LONDON AND NEW YORK

First published 2017
by Routledge
2 Park Square, Milton Park, Abingdon, Oxon OX14 4RN

and by Routledge
711 Third Avenue, New York, NY 10017

Routledge is an imprint of the Taylor & Francis Group, an informa business

British Library Cataloguing in Publication Data
A catalogue record for this book is available from the British Library

Library of Congress Cataloging in Publication Data
Names: Hillier, Liz, author.
Title: Make Key Stage 3 matter in English / Liz Hillier.
Description: Milton Park, Abingdon, Oxon; New York, NY: Routledge, 2017.
Identifiers: LCCN 2016048772 | ISBN 9781138208544 (hardback) |
ISBN 9781138208551 (pbk.) | ISBN 9781315458939 (ebook)
Subjects: LCSH: Language arts (Secondary)–Great Britain. |
English language–Study and teaching (Secondary)–Great Britain.
Classification: LCC LB1631 .H514 2017 | DDC 428.0071/20941–dc23
LC record available at https://lccn.loc.gov/2016048772

ISBN: 978-1-138-20854-4 (hbk)
ISBN: 978-1-138-20855-1 (pbk)
ISBN: 978-1-315-45893-9 (ebk)

Typeset in Melior
by Deanta Global Publishing Services, Chennai, India

This book is dedicated to the courage and resilience of Bethan and James who have taught me that anything is possible if you put your mind to it.

Contents

Acknowledgements

It is said that we all have a book inside of us; I would never have guessed for one moment that mine would be about the importance of KS3 English in the National Curriculum for England. This is a subject that I have been passionate about for as long as I have been teaching and there are many people who I need to thank for helping me get to this point.

Firstly, I want to thank my editor, Annamarie Kino, as without her this book would never have happened. Also, I would like to thank Sarah Richardson, who has been extremely supportive over the past six months, especially during the times when I was overloaded with schoolwork and trying to figure out how to write a book at the same time!

Being part of the Suffolk KS3 English working group were the best two years of my career. Thank you to Jo Merrion for bringing all of us kindred spirits together in the same room. I can't wait to work with all of the following outstanding English teachers again in the future – Caroline Francis, Susan MacGregor, Naomi Peirson, Clare Morris and James Thurlbourn.

The KS3 English curriculum model that I am proposing would not have evolved at all if it was not for the support of the outstanding English department at Claydon High School in Suffolk. I am extremely lucky to be part of a team that is generous with its time and collaborative in its approach to helping the pupils in our school to be the best they can be. Thank you Maeve Taylor, Carrie Chittock, Rachel Duxbury, Amanda Maton, Alice Longden, Christine Leggett and Kim Brand for readily taking on the challenges that this proposed KS3 English curriculum model has presented over the past three years.

I would like to say a very special thank you to my Head of Department, Julia Simpson, who works tirelessly to make sure that we have an outstanding English department in our school. Since January 2014 you have been with me every step of the way on this KS3 English curriculum journey and have trusted me and my ideas which, at times, have required a leap of faith! I also want to pay a special tribute to Leonie Crissell and Sarah Lovell-Brown, who have flown with the ideas that they have been presented with in this proposed KS3 English curriculum model. Their contributions to the model and their innate sense of the importance of collaborative working have played a vital part in the way the model has evolved. I particularly look forward to making more training videos with Sarah. Not only was the Socratic discussion video great fun to make, it has also provided an excellent in-house CPD training for the department.

I also want to say thank you to Alice Martin, who is not only an inspiring design and technology teacher, but is also passionate about making sure that literacy is embedded across the curriculum. She is also a very good friend who has been extremely supportive during this book-writing process. The staff at Combs Middle School in Suffolk, especially those who fully supported the cross-curricular writing project between 2007 and 2008, all deserve my personal thanks. It is hard to believe that Combs has now closed like so many middle schools over the past five years; especially when recalling the teamwork and excellent teaching and learning that took place in the school during my tenure as Head of English.

Professor Debra Myhill is someone whom I fervently admire and during my career her courses and seminars have inspired me to go into my own classroom and try lots of different approaches to learning that previously I may not have had the confidence to try. I feel privileged that Debra has taken the time out of her busy schedule over the past twelve months to read through the various stages of my book proposal. I also can't thank her enough for taking the time to look at my resources during conferences that we have attended together and for providing me with constructive feedback.

It always feels like such a cliché to thank family and friends, but I can categorically state that their unrelenting support and help has made this process that much easier. I would especially like to thank my friend Helen Lawrence for her amazing command of the English language and the advice that she has given me along the way. My husband, Rob Hillier, who has also doubled up as my illustrator, has given me the space that I have needed to write this book – thank you for giving me that gift of time, especially as we both know from firsthand experience just how precious it is. Throughout my life, there is one woman who has never let me give up on my dreams. Not only is Alice Kirwin my mum, but she is also the strongest woman I know. Like the true Mancunian women that we are, we will always passionately stand up for what we believe in.

Abbreviations used in this book

APP	Assessing Pupils' Progress
CPD	Continuing Professional Development
DFE	Department for Education *(2010 to present)*
DFES	Department for Education and Skills *(2001–2007)*
DCSF	Department for Children, Schools and Families *(2007–2010)*
EBacc	English Baccalaureate
EHCP	Educational Health Care Plan
GCSE	General Certificate of Secondary Education
HLTA	High Level Teaching Assistants
HMI	Her Majesty's Inspectorate
LAC	Literacy across the Curriculum
LWL	Life without Levels
LWSL	Life without Sub-Levels
NC	National Curriculum
NQT	Newly Qualified Teacher
OFSTED	Office for Standards in Education, Children's Services and Skills
OFQUAL	Office of Qualifications and Exam Regulation
PLTS	Personal Learning and Thinking Skills
PPA	Planning, Preparation and Assessment
SATs	Standard Assessment Tests
SEN	Special Educational Needs
SMSC	Spiritual, Moral, Social and Cultural Development
SPAG	Spelling, Punctuation and Grammar
SPLD	Specific Learning Difficulty
VLE	Virtual Learning Environment

The importance of Key Stage 3 English

Since its statutory inception in 1988, the National Curriculum has evolved, changed and been slimmed down on many occasions by different governments. In the fourteen years since I started my career as an English teacher, I have experienced three of these 'new' National Curriculum models; each of which has claimed to be better than its predecessor in preparing our young people for the rigours of real life outside school.

The significance of these two parallel timelines is this: at no point has the importance of KS3, in particular KS3 English, been at the heart of a publication that can advise teachers and departments how to: (1) Make KS3 English matter in their school and (2) Design a robust KS3 English curriculum model that can evolve and withstand change according to the dictates on a national level.

From my fledgling years as a trainee teacher and an NQT it was clear that the lack of KS3 English was not because teachers weren't enthused about developing an interesting and evolving curriculum. Ultimately, the problem lay in its place in the order of the National Curriculum. Nestled comfortably between KS2 and KS4, KS3 English often feels more like a buffer zone between those pupils who have completed their statutory primary curriculum and those at the end of their compulsory secondary school journey.

Furthermore, my KS3 English training focused largely on the two key scenes from the Shakespeare Year 9 SATs, as these statutory tests were used as a standardised measure of how successful the buffer zone curriculum had been for Year 9 pupils. This intensive SATs preparation, alongside the starter-middle-plenary format as advocated and pressed by the National Literacy Strategy, meant that my formative training and early years of teaching KS3 English was marred by a national political agenda that wanted to drive standards upwards regardless of its detriment to imagination and enjoyment.

As the years have marched on and the pressure on KS2 SATs results and pupil progress at GCSE has become more intense, it is more imperative than ever that schools design a robust KS3 English curriculum model – a model which successfully builds on the skills taught and learned in KS2, whilst also preparing the pupils over the three years for the assessments that they will sit for at the end of KS4, whatever these assessments may or may not look like in the future. In terms of the latter Key Stage, a robust and rigorous KS3 English curriculum will ensure that departments across the country can avoid the annual firefighting at KS4 where teachers, pupils and resources are stretched to such an extent that there is the inevitable burn-out in the middle of June.

Ofsted's inflammatory report and claim that KS3 is the 'poor relation' to KS4

On 10 September 2015, Ofsted finally verbalised and laid down written authority to the idea that KS3 mattered by refuting this perceived metaphorical buffer zone status and by giving credence to the idea that it is the pivotal Key Stage in a pupil's statutory education. Ultimately, Ofsted suggests that for a student to succeed at KS4, they have to experience an engaging three years at KS3. On the day of its release, the report *Key Stage 3: The wasted years*[1] caused a crucible of educational debate to bubble over, with all sides who had a vested interest in the report's findings commenting on its content and, specifically, its damning title. Apart from the title, more scathing and incendiary comments are made in the opening stages of the report, as KS3 is described metaphorically as 'the poor relation' to KS4 in the report's executive summary (Ofsted: 2015).

Whatever side of the debate a teacher, pupil or parent may find themselves on, the fact that for a brief moment in September 2015 a lively, impassioned discussion ensued about whether KS3 in general mattered and was prioritised in schools across England was certainly well received by me, not only as an English teacher in Ipswich, Suffolk who has always been passionate about the importance of KS3 English in a pupil's educational life, but also as the mother of two young children, one of whom has specific learning difficulties (SPLD), who are embarking on their statutory educational journey. Hopefully this refreshing educational debate about KS3, and in particular KS3 English, will continue to be at the forefront of educational discussion and not lost amongst other political education agendas that are often thrust into the national media limelight.

On that day in early September 2015 *Key Stage 3: The wasted years?* was certainly a burning educational topic, provoking lots of different responses to the survey and its subsequent report which had been commissioned by Her Majesty's Chief Inspector at the time, Sir Michael Wilshaw. Previously, in his Annual Report 2013–2014 Sir Michael noted that 'Eighty-two per cent of primary schools are now good or outstanding' compared to '71%' in secondary schools. He continued that this figure of 71% was 'no better'[2] than the figure quoted regarding the percentage of good or outstanding secondary schools in his previ-

2

ous Annual Report 2012–2013.[3] The need to examine the reasons behind this plateau in terms of secondary school performances in England helped spearhead the 2014–2015 Her Majesty's Inspectorate (HMI) survey, so that Ofsted could:

get an accurate picture of whether Key Stage 3 is providing pupils with suffi- cient breadth and challenge, and helping them to make the best possible start to their secondary education.

(Ofsted: 2015)

How does this book address the issues raised in Ofsted's 2015 report?

In terms of the finer details of the *Key Stage 3: The wasted years?* report and its *Executive Summary*, specifically those of concern to KS3 English and how these aspects have an impact on the building of a robust KS3 English curricu- lum model – the aspects of which are examined throughout this book – the findings are as follows:

- 'In one in five of the routine inspections analysed', inspectors raised 'con- cerns … particularly in relation to the slow progress made in English … and the lack of challenge for the most able pupils'. These are issues that will be addressed in Chapter 4 of this book: 'Inclusion and Challenging the Most Able in KS3 English.'
- School leaders 'staffed Key Stages 4 and 5 before Key Stage 3' and 'As a result, some Key Stage 3 classes were split between more than one teacher or were taught by non-specialists.' In the final report, 'non-specialists' are defined by Ofsted as 'a teacher who does not have that subject as part of their undergraduate or teaching qualification.' The implications of which will be looked at in further detail in Chapter 2: 'Developing the Planning Cycle for Key Stage 3 English.'
- 'Too many secondary schools did not work effectively with partner prima- ry schools to understand pupils' prior learning and ensure that they built on this during Key Stage 3.' This will be the focus of Chapter 5: 'Planning for English Transition Across the Primary and Secondary Phase.'

In addition to the report's executive summary, the specific elements pertaining to KS3 English in the report's 'Key Findings' section are that:

- 'Many secondary schools do not build sufficiently on pupils' prior learn- ing', with pupil responses to inspectors indicating 'that repeating work is more of an issue in mathematics and English than in the foundation subjects'. Within Chapter 2, 'Developing the Planning Cycle for Key Stage 3 English', there will be examples of models of long-, medium- and short-term planning that suggest ways in which all pupils have the opportunity to build on prior learning.

- 'Developing pupils' literacy skills in Key Stage 3 is a high priority in many schools.' The fact that 'literacy', 'high priority' and 'many schools' are mentioned in the same sentence is extremely positive and all English teachers should take some comfort from the fact that colleagues in other subject areas are helping us transfer those crucial reading and writing skills. In Chapter 6, 'LAC and SPAG: Divisive or Cohesive Abbreviations in the KS3 English Curriculum?', I will look at the two acronyms independently of each other and then together, and the implications that both have in terms of continuing to build positive relationships between English and other areas of the curriculum.

- 'Homework is not consistently providing the opportunities for pupils to consolidate or extend their learning in Key Stage 3. Approximately half of the pupils who responded to the online questionnaire said that their homework never, or only some of the time, helps them to make progress.' KS3 English teachers across England frequently blog and are active in Internet forums discussing the pros and cons of the different types of homework that should be set, especially at KS3. In Chapter 9, 'Key Stage 3 English Homework', I will demonstrate examples of the ways in which meaningful homework can be embedded in terms of the wider KS3 English curriculum.

Although a number of these key findings have been quantified and qualified within the survey conducted by Ofsted through interviews, lesson observations and an appendix dedicated to successful case studies, there are parts of a rigorous KS3 English curriculum for the twenty-first century that have been overlooked: namely the fact that the importance of media in the KS3 English Curriculum and specifically the importance of media texts in helping improve a pupil's speaking and listening, reading and writing is notably absent from the report's executive summary and key findings. This may be attributed to the fact that within the *English programmes of study: Key Stage 3*[4] there is no explicit reference to how media texts can be used successfully to support the transferability of speaking and listening, reading and writing skills.

There has been no controlled assessment or explicit component on media studies in the English language GCSE since 2010. Furthermore, many schools are dropping GCSE media studies as it is regarded as a 'soft' subject and won't contribute to the academic English Baccalaureate (EBacc) which schools are to be judged on in the future. I find this extremely concerning and have raised the issue in Chapter 8: 'Using Multimodal Texts in Key Stage 3 English'. This chapter will clearly demonstrate how media texts need to be taught explicitly and implicitly in any KS3 English curriculum model, regardless of KS4 measurements. There will be examples of how to put multimodal texts into KS3 English long- and medium-term plans over the three years. In particular, I will show how multimodal texts can be used with reluctant readers so that they can build their confidence when transferring the skills of reading to any text-type that they are given.

The unions' response to Ofsted's 2015 report, *Key Stage 3: The wasted years?*

As well as omissions from key areas within the curriculum, such as media studies, the report also received criticism from the major teaching unions. The General Secretary of the Association of Schools and Colleges (ASCL), Brian Lightman, asserted on the day of the report's release that the title *Key Stage 3: The wasted years?* was 'negative', especially as he and his union believed that the report 'actually contains much evidence of good practice',[5] which is true, especially as there is an appendix of good practice that supplements the survey's findings and constructively contributes to the final report. According to Ofsted, the eight case studies that are featured in the report's appendix show 'examples of practice that schools indicated were having a positive impact on their pupils'[6] and seems to validate Mr Lightman's view that not all Key Stage Three teaching is '*wasted*' (Ofsted: 2015).

Furthermore, whilst unions such as the Association of Teachers and Lecturers (ATL) seem to appreciate the report's belief that more needs to be done *to improve* transition between Year 6 and Year 7, Dr Mary Boulsted, the Union's General Secretary, raises the practical concerns that seem to be omitted from the final report – namely, 'the context within which secondary school leaders and teachers are working'.[7] This sentiment is echoed across many of the main teaching unions in terms of their responses to the survey and report; the 'context' and the concerns which arise every day can be summarised in a simple list: teacher retention, recruitment shortage, staff shortages, excessive workload, performance-related pay and the rapid introduction of a new National Curriculum and statutory testing in the primary sector, as well as the introduction of new GCSEs at Key Stage 4.

With regards to the latter, the new GCSEs for English language and English literature have been the toughest in a generation and provide most concern and stress for the secondary school English teacher on a daily basis. The rapidity with which these curriculum and assessment changes have been made and implemented over the past five years seems to add substance to the overall collective view from the unions that KS3 will naturally slide down the ladder in terms of priority for secondary schools because so much of their judgement is based on GCSE results and the performance of their pupils when they have a Section 5 inspection.

In terms of prioritising one Key Stage over the other in English there seems to be a 'which came first?' scenario: the chicken or the egg? Because, aside from the politics and KS3 English policies that are being discussed and implemented at a national level, there is an appetite amongst those of us at the chalk face to discuss why KS3 seems to be regarded as the 'poor relation' (Ofsted: 2015) by those of us in the profession and more importantly what can we do to raise its status and make it equally as important as KS4, especially as a robust, engaging and evolving curriculum at KS3 English can help cement the foundations that young people will need as they begin their exam specifications in Year 10.

Moreover, whether any GCSEs in English Language and English literature take this current, 100% closed-book exam approach or not, a successful KS3 English curriculum model will be able to work with major changes to any new National Curriculum and provide the pupils with the English skills that they need to sit any Year 11 English language or literature exam that they will undertake – whatever format they may adopt in the future.

'No more firefighting at KS4 English'

My initial title for this book was 'No more firefighting at KS4 English', as this was the name of a presentation that I had delivered at a county-wide conference alongside five colleagues and outstanding teachers from across Suffolk who are also passionate about raising the profile of KS3 English. This working group was initially brought together by the then County Advisor for Secondary English in order to respond to the findings from the 2012 Ofsted Report, *Moving English forward*[8] which set out to answer the question, 'how can attainment in English be raised to move English forward in schools?' (Ofsted: 2015). By collaborating and working closely together over a period of two and a half years, it meant that we were given the opportunity to work on practical strategies that would help move KS3 English forward across our own schools. We were so heartened by this collaboration that we wanted to share these strategies and ideas with other schools, which we did during two conferences in 2014 and 2015.

Although 'No more firefighting at KS4 English' is a laboured title that doesn't happily roll off the tongue, I firmly stand by its sentiment that a robust and dynamic KS3 English curriculum will mean no more firefighting at KS4. Furthermore, since I was a trainee teacher, I have always believed that not only is every child in England entitled to a three-year KS3 National Curriculum in English by law, they are also entitled to access a KS3 English curriculum that excites and challenges them; that fires their imagination and erodes passive learning; that doesn't simply prepare them for the GCSE English language and English literature exams, but prepares them to question the world in which they live so that they are more rounded individuals when they enter the workplace. Schools shouldn't feel they have to start the students' GCSEs in English a year early; rather they should place an equal amount of importance on the KS3 English curriculum in Year 9 and on considering the ways in which it can successfully transition into Year 10.

In this book I provide credible suggestions about how to help departments improve their KS3 English model, as I have been using and working with lots of these ideas throughout my teaching career successfully. Even though I have had the pressures of A-Level and GCSE classes to contend with over the last fourteen years, I have loved experimenting with different ideas in my KS3 planning and marking. Being inventive and creative with a willing audience of KS3 pupils often took the edge off the stresses of getting the older pupils the exam results that both they and the school needed. All of these ideas have influenced and shaped the suggested KS3 curriculum model that I am proposing. Finally, I hope that the fact that this book doesn't support either side of the political divide, and provides concrete help, support and anecdotal encouragement for fellow English teachers across England, will go some way in easing the pressures that we are all under whilst also showing that English at KS3 really does matter.

Notes

1 *Key Stage 3: The wasted years?* Ofsted, September 2015; https://www.gov.uk/government/publications/key-stage-3-the-wasted-years.
2 *Ofsted Annual Report 2013/14: Schools report*, Ofsted, December 2014; https://www.gov.uk/government/publications/ofsted-annual-report-201314-schools-report.
3 *Ofsted Annual Report 2012/13: Schools report*, Ofsted, December 2013; https://www.gov.uk/government/publications/ofsted-annual-report-201213-schools-report.

4   *Statutory guidance: National curriculum in England: English programmes of study*, Department for Education, September 2013 (Updated, July 2014); https://www.gov.uk/government/publications/national-curriculum-in-england-english-programmes-of-study.

5   *Ofsted Key Stage 3 report is 'disappointing'*, Association of School and College Leaders, 2015; http://www.ascl.org.uk/news-and-views/news_news-detail.ofsted-key-stage-3-report-is-disappointing.html.

6   *Ofsted key stage 3 curriculum survey 2015: 8 good practice case studies*, Ofsted, September 2015; https://www.gov.uk/government/publications/ofsted-key-stage-3-curriculum-survey-2015-8-good-practice-case-studies.

7   *Ofsted's key stage 3 report is too simplistic and unfair on schools*, Association of Teachers and Lecturers (ATL), 2015; https://www.atl.org.uk/media-office/2015/Ofsteds-key-stage-3-report-is-too-simplistic-and-unfair-on-schools.asp.

8   *Moving English forward: Action to raise standards in English*, Ofsted, April 2013; https://www.gov.uk/government/publications/moving-english-forward.

Developing the planning cycle for Key Stage 3 English

It is difficult to comprehend how and where to start developing a KS3 English planning cycle when in the midst of an already overcrowded academic year: firstly, there are three years to plan for compared to only two at KS4 and secondly, it never feels like there will be enough time to complete what seems to be an enormous and overwhelming task. Whilst it is a daunting task, once you start drafting on paper and exorcising resources and schemes of work that are no longer fit for purpose, the trepidation steadily turns into anticipation and finally excitement as you see your KS3 English curriculum evolving.

The most important factors to a successful and robust KS3 English curriculum are collaboration and the process of continual reflection throughout the year about how successful the curriculum model in place is in terms of your department's goals, which are usually reviewed annually in the Departmental Development Plan. However, evaluation of the KS3 English schemes of work and assessments that are in place throughout the year is the most important part of the planning cycle. Without regular self-reflection and the willingness to reflect upon schemes of work termly, and specifically focusing on a KS3 English curriculum review on a yearly or bi-annual basis in addition to the time set aside for the Departmental Development Plan, it will be difficult to create a robust curriculum model that can withstand any future major changes at a national level.

Currently, the planning cycle that I have designed has taken the following format:

Whilst the individual schemes of work are reviewed by the department each term, the final evaluation of the success of the KS3 English curriculum is undertaken towards the end of the academic year so that any amendments and changes can be made to start with effect from the following September. One of the weaknesses identified by Ofsted in its September 2015 survey and report, *Key Stage 3: The wasted years*, is that there is a 'lack of priority given to Key Stage Three by many school leaders'.[1] Fortunately, this has not been my experience, especially in terms of the time that I have been allocated for the development of the planning cycle and KS3 English model that I have implemented at my current school. Indeed, the success of how engaging this particular model and cycle is has relied solely on the understanding by all involved that KS3 English is as important as that at KS4.

Stage One: KS3 English curriculum review

Initially, in January 2014 a colleague and I were given two days off timetable to begin discussing what resources we already had and how they might fit into the curriculum model that I was proposing. Being given the time to do this during peak KS4 firefighting time was a bold move, but the long-term benefits of taking this time to move on with the KS3 English curriculum far outweighed the short-term loss of time at KS4. Throughout the spring and summer terms of 2015 I was also given extra PPA time to work on specific schemes of work which was also extremely useful. However, the reality is that there will never be enough time to get everything right all at once. I have dedicated many nights and weekends to working on this curriculum model, but the trade-off is already paying huge dividends as the model is malleable and is able to change shape as and when is needed – much more easily than if there was a static KS3 English model in place that only changed once there had been a huge shift in policy at a national level every four to five years.

Regarding how successful the model has been in preparing our pupils for the rigors of GCSE English language and literature in terms of valued added and pupil progress, this can only be measured when the year seven cohort that began the cycle for the first time two years ago completes their KS4 exams in three years' time. If in that time there is a major shift in policy towards KS3 English at national level, then a robust curriculum model such as this one that I am proposing, which regularly evaluates and reflects upon its successes and areas for development, will be able to withstand any national changes and will hopefully cause minimal disruption to the pupils. If a school only changes or adapts its KS3 English curriculum model every four to five years, then it is at risk of becoming reactionary.

In a time of uncertainty regarding the future of education in England, another important factor to consider when designing the new curriculum model was the issue of staffing KS3 English, especially during a time when there is a great deal of debate surrounding recruitment and retention of specialist English teachers. This is a universal issue and is also addressed in the *Key Stage 3: The wasted years?* report when, alarmingly, '85% of the leaders interviewed prioritised the staffing of Key Stage 4 and Key Stage 5 before Key Stage Three' (Ofsted: 2015). In a world where GCSE and A-Level league tables and value-added rule, especially in terms of the judgement of a school and its staff, then it is totally understandable that senior leaders make these difficult staffing decisions.

Prior to the confirmation of this staffing issue in the report, I had already decided back in January 2014 that any successful curriculum model would have to support the people who were actually going to end up standing in front of a classroom and delivering the KS3 English lessons on a day-to-day basis to Years 7, 8 and 9. In the section on 'Quality of instruction'[2] in *Learning for Mastery*, Benjamin S. Bloom, J. Thomas Hastings and George F. Madaus (1971, p. 47) state that, 'We believe if every student had a very good tutor, most of them would be able to learn a particular subject to a high degree'. In an ideal world there would be a subject specialist with the relevant qualifications in every English department across England to ensure that each pupil had the optimum chance to succeed in KS3 English.

Due to the fact that there is a recognised absence of fully qualified English teachers delivering KS3 lessons, then there has to be the availability of explicit planning for all of the department. Subsequently, I believe that my proposed curriculum model supports non-specialists, instructors, split classes and long-term supply teachers who are parachuted in to fill the KS3 English staffing gaps. These valuable members of the KS3 English team can be confident that they are following a meaningful plan of learning that has been carefully mapped out rather than a series of arbitrary worksheets and textbooks that keep the students occupied in the staffing hiatus interim.

Stage Two: Long-term planning

Year 1 long-term plan example

I designed the initial long-term plan for our new curriculum model on large pieces of A3 paper covered with lots of annotation before the initial meeting in January 2014. By doing this there was no sense of obligation to commit to the Autumn One, Autumn Two – Spring One, Spring Two – Summer One, Summer Two system that I was proposing across the three year groups, as it was in draft form and didn't have to be adhered to. Following discussion of this particular idea, it was agreed that we wanted to adopt this approach and teach the same thing at the same time across all three year groups so that (a) there was consistency for all members of the team, in particular non-specialist English teachers, newly qualified teachers and part-time staff and (b) teachers could share teaching ideas and good practice. An example from the final long-term plan for that first year can be seen in Figure 2.1. This diagram shows the Autumn 2 plan

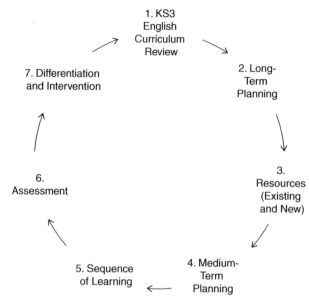

Figure 2.1 The KS3 English suggested planning cycle.

implemented for that first year which also coincided with the launch of the new National Curriculum.

There is a number of key features on Table 2.1 which demonstrate how, after that initial meeting in January 2014, we balanced existing schemes of work and resources, the new statutory requirements for spelling, punctuation and grammar (SPAG) and the need to address the sheer number of text types which had been stipulated within the 2014 National Curriculum Programmes of Study[3] for English in our final curriculum model. Furthermore, it was extremely important that the department didn't disregard the importance of skills-based learning – in particular, the personal, learning and thinking skills (PLTS) and especially the role of speaking and listening that had been a prominent part of the preceding 2010 National Curriculum: 'A Big Picture of the Secondary Curriculum.'[4] Within the 'Creativity'[5] section of the 2010 National Curriculum's 'Key Concepts', skills such as the ability to make 'fresh connections' between texts, 'inventive approaches to making meaning', 'using imagination to create themes', 'taking risks, playing with language', 'using imagination' and problem-solving would remain a major factor within our curriculum model, as these are the skills that enable the pupil to become an autonomous and responsible learner.

If the department had chosen to disregard these crucial life skills that had been a major focus in the preceding National Curriculum, it would mean that the pupils would have been subjected to a content-driven curriculum which didn't prepare them for the skills needed in the working world. It could be

Table 2.1 Year 1 long-term plan example.

	Key Stage Three English: 2014-2015: Autumn Two	
Year 7	**Year 8**	**Year 9**
Poetry	*Poetry*	*Poetry*
(4 Weeks)	(3 Weeks)	(4 weeks)
Unit Name: *Shaking Up the Senses!*	**Unit Name:** *Questioning the Voice in Contemporary Poetry*	**Unit Name:** *Why War?*
Cauldron of Characterisation	*Cauldron of Characterisation*	*Cauldron of Characterisation*
(3 Weeks)	(4 Weeks)	(3 Weeks)
Unit Name: *Will the real Scrooge please stand up?*	**Unit Name:** *Being a Detective!*	**Unit Name:** *It's All Elementary!*
Assessment Tasks for Autumn 2	**Assessment Tasks for Autumn 2**	**Assessment Tasks for Autumn 2**
1. Close analysis of a poem 2. S&L: Performance of a Ballad	1. Comparing and Contrasting the Poets' Voices in two Post-Modern Poems **(See MTP and Sequence of Learning for differentiated task)**	1. *Comparing and Contrasting values in the poetry of the First World War* **(See MTP and Sequence of Learning for differentiated task)**
SPAG Lesson Fortnightly: Sp: Securing Knowledge of Homophones and Greek Root Words P: Securing the accuracy of basic punctuation G: Pupils to be able to turn simple sentences into complex sentences.	**SPAG Lesson Fortnightly:** Sp: Securing knowledge of complex polysyllabic words by focusing on prefixes and suffixes P: Ensuring Accuracy and Variety G: Revising the appropriateness of syntax in formal and informal texts.	**SPAG Lesson Fortnightly:** Sp: Consolidation and secure knowledge of complex syllabic and irregular spelt words P: Consolidation and Secure knowledge of punctuation as well as using sophisticated punctuation techniques for effect in writing. G: Ensuring secure use of sentence variety to create certain effects in writing.
Text Types for A2: Novel, Poetry, Auto-biographical, Multi-Modal, Still Images, Biographical, Recount, Reports, Newspaper Articles	**Text Types for A2:** Poetry, Multi-Modal Texts, Reports, Newspaper Articles, Short Stories, Biographical, Autobiographical, Analytical Commentary, Still Images	**Text Types for A2:** Poetry, Propaganda, Multi-Modal Texts, Reports, Newspaper Articles, short stories, biographical, autobiographical, analytical commentary
PLTS: Let's Think in English Lesson: *Poetry or Prose?* Reasoning pattern: <u>Classification</u>	**PLTS:** Let's Think in English Lesson: *The Open Window.* Reasoning pattern: <u>Narrative Sequencing</u>	**PLTS:** Let's Think in English Lesson: *An Occurrence at Owl Creek Bridge* **(This lesson has since been transferred to the GCSE LTE programme)** Reasoning pattern: <u>Narrative Sequencing</u>
	Christmas Holidays	

Let's Think in English (LTE) is a teaching programme which helps students to develop the reasoning skills needed for success in English. It is a two-year programme of specially designed lessons intended to be delivered fortnightly. The programme has been developed since 2009, closely modelled on Adey and Shayer's Cognitive Acceleration in Science Education (CASE). As with CASE, lessons were first developed for Key Stage 3, but separate suites of lessons have been developed for Key Stages 1 and 2 and for Key Stage 4 (GCSE).

Laurie Smith and Michael Walsh (King's College, London: August 2016)
www.letsthinkinenglish.org

Figure 2.2

suggested that a content-driven curriculum reduces the value of the speaking and listening skills that the pupils will need later in life. The importance of *Speaking and Listening in the KS3 Curriculum* and the significant part that the *Let's Think in English*[6] (see Figure 2.2) lessons play in our curriculum model will be addressed in detail in Chapter 7.

Year 2: Long-term plan example

During the two-day KS3 English departmental review that took place in July 2015, nearly 18 months after our first curriculum overhaul, a number of findings and recommendations were made in Section 2: '*Long-Term Planning and Staff Evaluations*' of a larger evaluative document that I had written. These included: more careful planning of assessments and their timings, as not all of them took place at the end of a scheme of work; how to map in library lessons so that they complemented the critical reading skills that were being taught in the KS3 English Classroom; and finally, and most crucially, highlighting on the long-term plan how the skills between each unit were being developed across Years 7, 8 and 9. For example, as Table 2.2 demonstrates, it was decided that it wasn't enough to say that all year groups would complete the 'Cauldron of Characterisation' units at the same time. From 2015 onwards, the department would know how the skills within that unit would develop from the revision of skills in Year 7 to a secure understanding of these skills in Year 9. During the 2015 two-day departmental review it was clear that the department needed to strengthen the way in which SPAG was being taught within (a) specific units of work and (b) exclusively outside the units of work. Therefore, it was decided that as a start to this SPAG review, skills progression would also be explicitly highlighted on the long-term plan for 2015–2016.

By adding these skill descriptors and inserting arrows to show explicitly how the pupils were expected to develop these specific skills over the three years, the department would not simply see the individual units in isolation of each other. Furthermore, by addressing the expected development of

Table 2.2 Year 2 long-term plan example.

Key Stage Three English: 2015–2016: Autumn Two		
Year 7	**Year 8**	**Year 9**
		Library Lesson: Year 9 Class Reader **Guided Reading Activities (Differentiated)**
Words, Sounds, Images Revision of Poetry Across Time: Medieval to the Victorians (4 Weeks) Unit Name: *Shaking Up the Senses!* (Writing/Reading to Inform/Describe/Entertain)	*Words, Sounds, Images* Revision and progression upon the different approaches to seen and unseen poetry (3 Weeks) Unit Name: *Questioning the Voice in Contemporary Poetry* (Writing/Reading to Inform/Describe/Entertain/Advise)	*Words, Sounds, Images* Secure knowledge of the different approaches to seen and unseen poetry (4 weeks) Unit Name: *Why War?* (Writing/Reading to Inform/Describe/Entertain/Persuade/Argue)
Cauldron of Characterisation Revision of the differences between direct and indirect characterisation with close attention to the language of Dickens (3 Weeks) Unit Name: *Will the real Scrooge please stand up?* (Writing to Review/Comment/Analyse)	*Cauldron of Characterisation* Analysis of a range of different characters across a range of short stories by Roald Dahl (4 Weeks) Unit Name: *Being a Detective!* (Writing to Review/Comment/Analyse)	*Cauldron of Characterisation* Secure knowledge and perceptive analysis of Conan-Doyle's Famous Detective (pre and post 20th-character evaluations of Sherlock Holmes) (3 Weeks) Unit Name: *It's All Elementary!* (Writing to Review/Comment/Analyse)
	Library Lesson: Year 8 Class Reader: **Guided Reading Activities (Already Differentiated)**	**Assessment Tasks for Autumn 2** 1. *Comparing and Contrasting values in the poetry of the First World War* (See MTP and Sequence of Learning for differentiated task)
	Library Lesson: Year 7 Group Readers: **Guided Reading Activities (Already Differentiated)**	
Assessment Tasks for Autumn 2: 1. Close analysis of a poem 2. S&L.: Performance of a Ballad	**Assessment Tasks for Autumn 2** 1. Comparing and Contrasting the Poets' Voices in 2. Post-Modern Poems (See MTP and Sequence of Learning for differentiated task: Close analysis of one poem)	
SPAG Lesson Fortnightly: Sp: Securing Knowledge of Homophones and Greek Root Words P: Securing the accuracy of basic punctuation G: Pupils to be able to turn simple sentences into complex sentences.	SPAG Lesson Fortnightly: Sp: Securing knowledge of complex polysyllabic words by focusing on prefixes and suffixes P: Ensuring Accuracy and Variety G: Revising the appropriateness of syntax in formal and informal texts.	SPAG Lesson Fortnightly: Sp: Consolidation and secure knowledge of complex syllabic and irregular spelt words P: Consolidation and Secure knowledge of punctuation as well as using sophisticated punctuation techniques for effect in writing. G: Ensuring secure use of sentence variety to create certain effects in writing.
Text Types for A2: Novel, Poetry, Autobiographical, Multi-Modal, Still Images, Biographical, Recount, Reports, Newspaper Articles	**Text Types for A2:** Poetry, Multi-Modal Texts, Reports, Newspaper Articles, Short Stories, Biographical, Autobiographical, Analytical Commentary, Still Images	**Text Types for A2:** Poetry, Propaganda, Multi-Modal Texts, Reports, Newspaper Articles, Short Stories, Biographical, Autobiographical, Analytical Commentary, Still Images
PLTS: Let's Think in English Lesson: *Jabberwocky* Reasoning Pattern: Classification	**PLTS:** Let's Think in English Lesson: *The Open Window.* Reasoning pattern: Narrative Seriation	**PLTS:** Let's Think in English Lesson: *The Last Days of Okawa* Reasoning pattern: Narrative Sequencing
	Christmas Holidays	

these skills on the long-term plan it would mean that any new members of staff, part-time staff or non-specialist English teachers would clearly be able to understand the overarching context of what was being taught, when it was being taught and why it was being taught.

Year 3: Long-term plan example

The most recent review of the KS3 English curriculum model has seen even more evolution in the long-term plan, which will commence in September 2016 and is based on a departmental collaborative discussion throughout the year in terms of what we deem to be our priorities for KS3 English for 2016–2017. For example, when comparing the Autumn 2 long-term planning in Table 2.1 to the most recent Autumn 2 long-term plan in Table 2.3, then there are a number of significant amendments which clearly demonstrate how the curriculum model has evolved in response to departmental and national priorities.

The first of these changes on Table 2.3 is the movement of text types from a discrete box of their own into the actual unit of work. For example, in the Autumn 2 Year 9 Unit, *War: What is it good for?* The text types: *Multi-Modal, Still Images, Report, Recount, Biography, Propaganda, Speech, WW1 Poetry, Timelines, Letters* and *Commentary* are now written alongside the unit name and skill descriptors. Previously the text types for the half-term had been allocated a unique area on the long-term plan because in the early stages of our KS3 English planning it was essential that the department clearly addressed the wide number of statutory text types from the new National Curriculum Programmes of Study, as Tables 2.2 and 2.4 demonstrate. Although they have been moved from a discrete box of their own, this does not mean that the need to address the different text types has diminished – simply it shows that after two years of teaching this new National Curriculum the department is confident that it is teaching the breadth of text types required – the specific text types have naturally migrated to the scheme of work where they belong.

Setting aside a unique area on the most recent KS3 English long-term plan (see Table 2.3) for the GCSE Assessment Objectives may seem to contradict the importance of teaching skills in our curriculum model. However, by labelling the GCSE Assessment Objectives on the long-term plan, it does not mean that they directly affect the teaching of our Years 7–9 schemes of work. On the contrary, the reference to the Assessment Objectives in our most up-to-date long-term plan is to remind staff that there is an opportunity to explicitly teach the exam techniques that they will need in Years 10 and 11. Therefore, these are the specific Assessment Objectives that they should be covering so that there is consistency across KS3 English

Table 2.3 Year 3 long-term plan example.

Key Stage Three English: 2016-2017: Autumn Two

Year 7	Year 8	Year 9
Words, Sounds, Images Revision of Poetry Across Time: Medieval to the Victorians (4 Weeks + 3Weeks A1)	*Words, Sounds, Images* Revision and progression upon the different approaches to seen and unseen poetry (3 Weeks+3Weeks A1)	*Words, Sounds, Images* Secure knowledge of the different approaches to seen and unseen poetry (4 weeks+3Weeks A1)
Unit Name: *Shaking Up the Senses!* (**Text Types: Multi-Modal, Still Images, Pop Music Lyrics, Different Types of Poems**)	Unit Name: *Questioning the Voice in Contemporary Poetry* (**Text Types: Post-Modern Poetry, Multi-Modal, Still Images, Recount, Commentary, Autobiography**)	Unit Name: *Why War?* (**Text Types: Multi-Modal, Still Images, Report, Recount, Biography, Propaganda, Speech, WW1 Poetry, Timelines, Letters, Commentary**)
Cauldron of Characterisation Revision of the differences between direct and indirect characterisation with close attention to the language of Dickens (3 Weeks)	*Cauldron of Characterisation* Analysis of a range of different characters across a range of short stories by Roald Dahl (4 Weeks)	*Cauldron of Characterisation* Secure knowledge and perceptive analysis of Conan-Doyle's Famous Detective (pre and post 20th-century character evaluations of the representation of Sherlock Holmes) (3 Weeks)
Unit Name: *Will the real Scrooge please stand up?* (**Text Types: Multi-Modal, Still Images, Differentiated Prose, Script, Biography**)	Unit Name: *Being a Detective!* (**Text Types: Short Stories, Multi-Modal, Still Images, Biography, Newspaper Reports**)	Unit Name: *It's All Elementary!* (**Text Types: Multi-Modal, Still Images, Differentiated Prose, Biography, Newspaper Reports**)
SPAG Lesson: Weekly (A2) Sp: To Consolidate and Secure our knowledge of Year 3 – 6 Spelling Lists (***Challenge:** Spelling Challenge and Preparatory Spelling Bee List*) **P:** To revise different methods to avoid comma splicing **G:** To secure our understanding of: Relative clauses; Modal Verbs and Adverbs; Adverbials (**SEN:** Secure understanding of subject-verb-object)	**SPAG Lesson: Fortnightly (A2): Sp:** Securing knowledge of complex polysyllabic words by focusing on prefixes and suffixes (***Challenge:** Spelling Challenge and Preparatory Spelling Bee List*) **P:** Ensuring Accuracy and Variety **G:** Revising the appropriateness of syntax in formal and informal texts.	**SPAG Lesson: Fortnightly (A2): Sp:** Consolidation and secure knowledge of complex syllabic and irregular spelt words **P:** Consolidation and Secure knowledge of punctuation as well as using sophisticated punctuation techniques for effect in writing. **G:** Ensuring secure use of sentence variety to create certain effects in writing.
Assessment Tasks for Autumn 2: Speaking and Listening: / *Group Performance of a Ballad*	**Assessment Tasks for Autumn 2** Writing: *Write the opening paragraphs for a detective story* (See Sequence of Learning for differentiated task)	**Assessment Tasks for Autumn 2** Reading: *Comparing and Contrasting values in the poetry of the First World War* (See Sequence of Learning for differentiated tasks)
GCSE Assessment Objectives Covered: Language: Writing: Paper 1: Imaginary Writing (AO5) **Reading:** Close Analysis of Language and Structure (AO2)	**GCSE Assessment Objectives Covered: Language: Writing: Paper 1:** Imaginary Writing (AO5/AO6) **Reading:** Close Analysis of Language and Structure (AO2) **Literature:** Poetry Comparison (AO1 and AO2)	**GCSE Assessment Objectives Covered: Language: Writing:** Paper 2: Writing to Inform/Explain (AO5 and AO6) **Reading:** Close Analysis of Language/Structure (AO2) **Literature:** Contextual Poetry Comparison (AO2 and AO3)
PLTS: Let's Think in English Lesson: *Jabberwocky* Reasoning Pattern: Classification (**Withdrawn from the LTE Programme. As such, will change in 2017 review**)	**PLTS:** Let's Think in English Lesson: *The Open Window.* Reasoning pattern: Narrative Sequencing	**PLTS:** Let's Think in English Lesson: *The Last Days of Okawa* Reasoning pattern: Narrative Sequencing

Library Lesson: Year 7 Group Readers: **Guided Reading Activities (Differentiated)**

Library Lesson: Year 8 Class Reader: **Guided Reading Activities (Differentiated)**

Library Lesson: Year 9 Class Reader **Guided Reading Activities (Differentiated)**

Christmas Holidays

Due to the unfortunate nature of the new GCSEs being 100% exam based, not tiered and closed book, it means that a number of pupils with inefficient working memories will be at a disadvantage and teaching them the exam skills that they will need to achieve the highest grade they can is currently as important as teaching them the skills that they will need in the world of work. This is not to say that these Assessment Objectives will take precedence in any future KS3 English long-term planning, because if anything changes on a national level that might affect our pupils, then this ever-evolving curriculum model that I am proposing will be able to absorb any new changes and remain current and up to date.

A further significant change in Table 2.3 is the development of SPAG on the long-term plan. As the new Year 7s will be the first cohort to have completed the new KS2 English grammar, punctuation and spelling test which, unlike previous testing at the end of Year 6, now 'has a greater focus on knowing and applying grammatical terminology with the full range of punctuation tested',[7] the department is keen to make sure that we build on the explicit SPAG skills that they have already been taught. This is why the Year 7 SPAG section on our long-term plan on Table 2.3 is different from those on Tables 2.2 and 2.4. These skills will be explicitly taught on a weekly, as opposed to a fortnightly, basis and 'those pupils that do not meet the "working towards" standard', (DFE: March 2016) for example, if they are still working through the Year 3 and 4 spelling lists,[8] will be challenged regularly each term to meet the 'expected standard' (DFE: March 2016).

This development also coincides with some of the findings from the Year 2 departmental review, where it was clear that there were still opportunities within the curriculum model to strengthen and evolve the teaching of SPAG explicitly across KS3 English. As the new Year 7 cohort progresses through to Year 9, the current Year 8 and 9 SPAG foci on the most recent long-term plan will be phased out. Over the next two years further explicit weekly SPAG lessons will be built into the Year 8 and 9 long-term plan so that there is a clearer overview of how the pupils are provided with opportunities to build on all of their spelling, punctuation and grammar skills from the end of KS2 to the end of KS3. Further investigation of how SPAG works in this curriculum model will be examined in Chapter 6: 'LAC and SPAG: Divisive or Cohesive Abbreviations in the Key Stage 3 English Curriculum?'

Stage three: Resources (existing and new)

The next stage of the planning cycle (Figure 2.1) is to overhaul existing resources whilst including new resources to support the long-term plan. Certainly, the most time-consuming and laborious organisation of resources

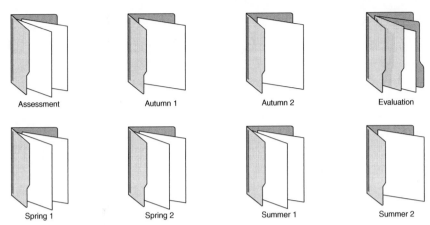

Figure 2.3 Illustration of arrangement of resources.

followed the planning of the very first curriculum model that was due to begin in 2014–2015. At that point members of staff were leaving and the department was preparing for new members who would join the team in September. Aside from this internal transition, there was also a great deal of uncertainty on a national level as to how pupils would be assessed in all Key Stages, so being practical and exorcising existing paper-based resources felt like yet another leap into the unknown. However, the fact that the long-term plan was in place by the summer term of May 2015 meant that the complete removal or development of existing resources could begin in earnest as collaborative discussions about what the department wanted to keep in the long term had already been established in the planning phase.

Clearing out drawers, emptying folders and rummaging through boxes was only one facet of this initial clear-out in the summer term of 2014. As well as organising hard copies of resources into clearly labelled trays and folders that complemented the long-term plan format, a number of resources were also kept virtually on the staff network shared area. I proposed that a reorganisation of the folders on the network was also needed to complement the curriculum model that was being developed.

Figure 2.3 shows the arrangement of the sub-folders within the main 'KS3 English Folder' on the staff network shared area which were and are currently arranged according to the: Autumn One, Autumn Two – Spring One, Spring Two – Summer One, Summer Two format that was clearly labelled on the long-term plan. Figure 2.3 also shows that there are two separate folders for 'Assessment' and 'Evaluation'. This decision was made so that these two areas of the curriculum model didn't detract from the main schemes of work as they are for collection of information and administrative purposes only.

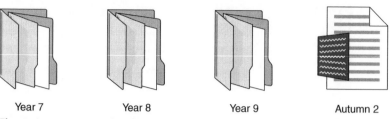

Year 7   Year 8   Year 9   Autumn 2

Figure 2.4 Arrangement of resources by year.

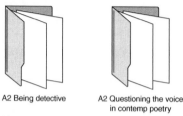

A2 Being detective   A2 Questioning the voice
                          in contemp poetry

Figure 2.5 Arrangement of resources by subject.

Figure 2.4 shows the Year 7, Year 8 and Year 9 sub-folders that can be found in the 'Autumn 2' Folder when clicked on by a member of staff – there is also a copy of the Autumn Two long-term plan. This particular figure clearly demonstrates the following: if a member of staff clicks on any of the folders in Figure 2.3, they can be reassured of a consistent approach to the organisation of virtual resources as it is an exact replicate of the sub-folders that can be found in Figure 2.4.

Finally, Figure 2.5 shows what happens if a member of staff clicks on 'Year 8' in Figure 2.4. They will find the two schemes of work, 'A2 Questioning the Voice in Contemporary Poetry' and 'A2 Being Detective', which are the schemes of work that correspond with the Autumn Two long-term plan. Once again this format is replicated across all of the folders found within Figures 2.3 and 2.4. In a scheme of work folder on the staff network shared area can be found the separate files, including the schemes' 'Middle Term Plan', 'Sequence of Learning', 'Resources', 'Suggested Assessment' and 'Homework Tasks' and a 'Pupil Self-Evaluation Form' (although it is now far easier to create an online survey that the students can access from their school e-mail). These virtual files are all replicates of the hard-copy resources that can be found in folders and trays in the departmental office. However, as teachers develop resources of their own that can be used in a particular scheme of work, it is much easier to slot them straight into a virtual folder online so that it can be incorporated into the scheme of work as that evolves.

Virtual Learning Environments (VLEs) and the increasing number of smartphones and tablets that help a teacher immediately connect with these online schemes of work mean that these virtual folders can be accessed from anywhere. Therefore, if a teacher takes a photograph of a setting or a sign that they feel will be of use in their teaching of a particular scheme of work, they can quickly add it to the designated folder on the VLE so that all members of the team can also access it rapidly and give feedback on how they have used it.

Organising the scheme of work folders so that they can evolve in a collaborative way has two major benefits. The first is that not only does the curriculum model evolve, but so does the collaborative pool of resources and the sharing of ideas that are at the heart of teaching and learning. The second major benefit is that by spending the time to organise all of the resources into the schemes of work for the year ahead, all staff in the department, whether they are existing members of the team or new to the school, newly qualified or trainee, non-specialist or part-time, have an equal opportunity to quickly and easily access the schemes of work and the corresponding resources.

Stage four: Medium-term planning

The most recent manifestation of the department's medium-term plan pro forma for the upcoming academic year can be seen in Table 2.4.

This medium-term plan has been developed in response to the feedback that has been given throughout the previous academic year in the departmental termly evaluations. The most significant change from our previous medium-term plan pro forma (2015–2016) to that exemplified in Table 2.4 is that there is a learning cycle which ensures that the teaching and learning of a scheme of work isn't arbitrarily linear, but follows a cycle in which students are given a clear opportunity to reflect upon what they have learned. By clearly identifying the different stages of the learning cycle in the medium-term plan, it means that all staff (whether they are subject specialists, part-time, newly qualified or not) are consistent in their response to the learning process.

This cycle also helps teachers to visualise where and when they should plan certain elements of the scheme of work depending on the class that is sitting in front of them. By following this cycle, it is hoped to encourage the teacher not to be too content driven in their individual planning but, instead, to focus on what content can be used to secure the learning of certain literary skills depending on the ability of the group that they teach. This complements the differentiation section of the medium-term plan where a number of examples of how to support and challenge the students is provided, although they do not necessarily need to be adhered to. Providing examples of differentiation within the scheme of work helps support non-specialists and newly qualified staff in their planning too – a more experienced and confident KS3 teacher will likely have their own differentiated approaches and would be encouraged to

Table 2.4 Example medium-term plan.

Autumn 1/2 Medium-Term Plan: **Year 9: *Words, Sounds, Images***	
Unit Name: Why War?	**Duration:** 7 Weeks: **A1** (3 Weeks) **A2** (4 Weeks)
Learning Cycle 5. Assessing 1: Knowledge 2. Skills → 1. KWHL 4. Feedback → 2. Different Text Types 3. Independent Learning	**Overview of unit (National Curriculum Subject Content):** Pupils will be expected to **(NC)** *Speak confidently and effectively through giving short speeches and presentations, expressing their own ideas and keeping to point.* Furthermore, they will have the opportunity to **(NC)** *participate in formal debates and structured discussions* whilst also being able to **(NC)** *improvise, rehearse and play scripts and poetry in order to discuss language use and meaning.* Pupils will secure their critical skills when recognising how **(NC)** *figurative language, vocabulary choice, grammar, text structure and organisational features, present meaning.* Furthermore, pupils will be expected to **(NC)** *write accurately, fluently and at length for pleasure and information* by **(NC)** *amending the vocabulary, grammar and structure of their writing to improve its coherence and overall effectiveness.*
1. **KWH**L (What do I **k**now? What do I **w**ant to know? **H**ow will I learn?)	*How confident am I with the close analysis of a variety of text types? *How well can I compare two texts whilst also forging a critical argument? *How will my existing knowledge of War, particularly World War One, help in my understanding of a writer's viewpoint and attitude? *How will I develop my empathy skills and understanding of war literature?
2. **Different Text Types**	Students begin to respond to the different elements within stage one of the learning cycle by responding to a range of different text types including: Multi-Modal, Still Images, Report, Recount, Biography, Propaganda, Speech, WW1 Poetry, Timelines, Letters, Commentary
3. **Independent Learning**	To work through the skills in the success criteria using a range of independent learning strategies including: active reading; summative tests such as: quizzes, word searches etc; formative self and peer-assessment of written work.
4. **Feedback**	Speaking and Listening: For example, Socratic discussion of issues within the literature studied; hot-seating of characters; tableaus.
5. **Assessing Knowledge and Skills**	Comparative Essay; Close analysis of a non-fiction text (See *Sequence of Learning* for details of tasks)
6. KWHL (What have I **l**earned during this unit?)	Response to stage one of the learning cycle; response to success criteria; create a summary/poster/poem about *what I have learned during this unit.*
Success Criteria	

- To **explore** how writers of the war genre use a range of techniques, including writing and sentence choices, to affect the reader (**Low Level Skill**)
- To **experimen**t with language and sentence styles appropriate to the war genre in creative writing and analytical writing (**Mid-Level Skill**)
- To **evaluate** and **critically choose** from a range of imaginative, flexible sentence structures to use for deliberate effect in both creative and analytical writing (**High-Level Skill**)

Table 2.4 (Continued).

Differentiation	
Support	*All paper resources to be on cream/light blue paper with a minimum of 12+ Comic Sans/Arial font-type and all projected resources to be on a cream/light blue background with Comic Sans/Arial font-type set at a minimum of 28+ with fewer words and symbols/images to support key words, terms and ideas for those pupils who experience a barrier to reading written texts. *Guided and independent reading using fiction and non-fiction cue cards: Focus on word level, working up to sentence level questions and tasks in guided reading groups. Even within the lower sets, the pupils will be grouped according to ability with colour-coded tasks to support differentiation *The provision of writing frames in extended writing tasks *Adopting roles in speaking and listening tasks that students feel confident with. *Socratic dialogue to boost confidence in formal group discussion as the pupils are there to support each other. Although the teacher may choose a straight forward class debate arrangement to encourage discussion as this is a more familiar discursive set-up. *Active reading strategies to help the pupils engage with unseen texts. *There is an alternative scheme of work available in this unit that is specifically designed to help pupils consolidate what they have learned at a steady pace. However, pupils will also be able to access a whole range of differentiated resources within the main sequence of learning as well. *The reading assessment is clearly structured with prompts and focuses on the close analysis **of one poem.**
Challenge	*Guided and independent reading using fiction and non-fiction cue cards: pupils to focus on sentence and text level questions and tasks. **Choice and Challenge:** Pupils to independently choose from a number of colour-coded guided questions and activities from across the range of guided and independent reading fiction and non-fiction cue cards. *Pupils will have the option to choose from a range of challenge activities in lessons and for homework. *Pupils will be grouped for guided reading and writing tasks according to their confidence and ability; however, there will be a great deal of focus on independent learning during sustained pieces of writing. *The reading assessment has few prompts and asks to compare two poems in detail. *All pupils are encouraged to vary their roles in Socratic discussion to develop their speaking and listening skills.

SPAG	**Sp**: Consolidation and secure knowledge of complex syllabic and irregular spelt words **P**: Consolidation and Secure knowledge of punctuation as well as using sophisticated punctuation techniques for effect in writing. **G:** Ensuring secure use of sentence variety to create certain effects in writing.
PLTS (Mandatory: To take place at the beginning of the sequence of learning)	Let's Think in English Lesson: The Last Days of Okawa. Reasoning pattern: Narrative Sequencing; Socratic Discussion
Links to other areas of the Curriculum:	History/Geography/PSHE/Religious Studies/Science/Art
Homework	See *Sequence of Learning*
SMSC: This Scheme of Work prepares our young people to move into the world of work and function fully as citizens to their community in which they live by:	Exploring experiences and respecting the values of others whilst also discovering themselves and the surrounding world and their place within it. They will be asked to respond to the array of texts with creativity and reflection including being able to recognise right from wrong and understanding the consequences of the choices that they may make. This scheme of work also promotes the British values of democracy, individual liberty and mutual respect and tolerance The unit coincides with the Royal British Legion's *Festival of Remembrance* marking the armistice of the First World War on November 11th.
Gender	It is easy to assume that the 'war' genre is stereotypically preferred by boys. However, this scheme of work begins by looking at the effects of war on all children who experience such horrors both a hundred years ago and presently in places such as the Middle East. All pupils will be required to develop their empathy skills and understand the suffering and hope that takes place by children who find themselves in a war-torn situation. They will also learn about the loss of a generation in Britain that took place exactly 100 years ago by looking at two First World War poetry anthologies from the perspective of both male and female writers.

share these collaboratively with the department. The success criteria and the different levels of skills such as those outlined in Table 2.4 also help students of all abilities to succeed at a certain level.

Elements of the long-term plan such as the different text types, PLTS and the formative assessment (if there is one in that particular scheme of work) are carried through to the medium-term plan as well as the strands of the statutory National Curriculum Subject Content in England (DFE: July 2014) that will be addressed within the scheme of work. Whole-school priorities also feature on the medium-term plan such as: how the scheme of work will link to other areas of the curriculum; how the scheme of work will ensure that there is a gender balance in terms of subject interest and accessibility; how the scheme of work will fit in with the school's policy on spiritual, moral, social and cultural development (SMSC), which is also a national priority too.

As with the long-term plan, the medium-term plan pro forma is evaluated termly through teacher feedback, with a final decision as to whether or not to amend it in the final KS3 English departmental review towards the end of the academic year when departmental priorities for the year ahead are discussed because we are allocated the time to discuss collaborative feedback; it is not too arduous to amend any planning if it is needed. Having tried previously to change a KS3 English curriculum and its long-, medium- and short-term planning on a four- to five-yearly basis in line with national changes, it proved to be far more time-consuming than being allocated the time to review it more frequently on an annual (or, more preferably, bi-annual) basis.

Stage five: Sequence of learning

From our very first meeting about how the KS3 English curriculum model would look, the decision was made to no longer use the phrase 'Short-Term Plan' across the department as it was deemed that short-term planning is the responsibility of the individual teacher. Rather, the term 'Sequence of Learning' was adopted, which outlines the differentiated learning objectives that must be covered throughout the scheme of work, alongside suggested teaching resources which might help the pupils successfully achieve the learning objectives. Table 2.5 is an example of what a KS3 English sequence of learning pro forma looks like: in this instance it shows the first week of a Year 9 poetry unit.

On the sequence of learning, it is the first column which is the most important, as it is the mandatory set of learning objectives that staff are expected to cover with their pupils during the scheme of work. However, like the 'Success Criteria'

Table 2.5 Autumn term 1/2: Sequence of learning: Year 9 words, sounds images: Why war?

Week	Learning Objectives	Suggested Resources to help fulfil the Week's Learning Objectives	Suggested Homework
1	PLTS: Let's Think Lesson: *The Last Days of Okawa* Reasoning pattern: Narrative Sequencing (Mandatory Lesson and PPT on VLE)		
	1. To **recall** any knowledge that the pupil may have on war photography or war literature (**Low-Level Skill**) 2. To **compare** and **contrast** different war photographs (**Mid-Level Skill**) 3. To **construct** and self or peer **appraise** a piece of descriptive writing based on a war photograph using a sensory language criterion (**High-Level Skills**)	• **KWHL** (What do I **k**now? What do I **w**ant to know? **H**ow will I **l**earn?) These grids can take any form that the teacher thinks will work best for their class (E.G. In their exercise books; on A3 paper hanging from learning lines using post-it notes; using ICT) This can be individual/paired/ group work with feedback. Make sure that the last column is clear ready to be completed at the end of the unit (NB. This column can also be completed alongside the student's learning journey too as part of a plenary activity). • **Famous War Photographs:** See the *Staff Shared Network* area for suggested pictures. There is a sample from famous paintings through to WW1 photography through to contemporary war pictures in more recent history) Students to question the pictures (**Differentiation: Support:** Provide examples of questions that the students may ask. **Challenge:** Students to focus on the higher-level questioning such as *how?* and *why?* In groups students to answer each other's questions. • **Descriptive Writing:** Students to choose one of the photographs and zoom in, using sensory language to describe what they see (**Differentiation: Support:** Writing Frames with one assigned picture. **Challenge:** Students to use two pictures and work on sophisticated juxtaposition of images) • **Homework feedback:** Hot seating activity: War Photographer	Prepare at least five questions (**Differentiation: Support:** Provide a couple of examples and then ask the students to write at least three questions. **Challenge:** With suggested answers) that you would like to ask a war photographer **Challenge:** Research a famous war photographer(s) and write a 200 word (300 words for comparative) summary **Challenge: And/or** Choose another picture that you have studied within the unit so far and either: write a further piece of descriptive writing and/or write a news-paper report to accompany the image.

outlined on the medium-term plan (Table 2.4), these are differentiated so that all students have the opportunity to successfully meet at least one of the learning objectives. In the second and third columns, 'Suggested Resources to help fulfil the Week's Learning Objectives' and 'Suggested Homework', the term 'Suggested' is used to mean just that: these ideas are only *suggested* and are not mandatory.

The number of suggested resources in the second column varies between each scheme of work. In Table 2.5 there is a high level of detail in terms of what suggested resources and ideas are available and this is due to the collaborative feedback and sharing of resources that has happened over the past two and a half years. There are also suggested ideas of how to differentiate some of the resources and teaching ideas in this column to encourage teachers to differentiate their activity depending on their group. Once again, a more experienced KS3 English teacher may have their own resources and ideas that will fit the weekly learning objective and once again these are encouraged to be shared collaboratively too.

It could be suggested that the level of detail in this column on Table 2.5 contradicts statements that have been made in the 'Medium-term planning' section of this chapter, whereby there is a conscious effort to ensure that teachers see the learning process that takes place as something cyclical and not (a) linear or (b) content driven. The final decision to have lots of suggested resources is linked back to the fact that there may be a non-specialist or newly qualified KS3 English teacher who may be delivering the subject matter for the very first time. It is important that these members of staff feel supported and have high-quality tools and resources to teach with whilst, at the same time, never assuming that a list of resources will mean that a teacher simply has something to deliver to their class – discussion with members of staff about how these resources work and how they may be delivered is something that needs to accompany the 'Sequence of Learning'.

As with the long-term and medium-term plans before it, the sequence of learning is regularly reviewed. In fact, it happens more frequently as staff are encouraged to drop any new resources, examples of pupils' work or any teaching ideas into the designated folder as they teach that particular scheme of work. Hard copies of the aforementioned go into the folders in the English office while any virtual copies simply slot into the online folders (Figure 2.5). The sequence of learning sections of the schemes of work are also discussed in more depth during the end-of-year KS3 English departmental review as it is highly likely that if changes are made to the long-term plan or medium-term plan (for example, the addition or removal of a formative assessment in a particular scheme of work), this will directly impact the sequence of learning.

Stage six: Assessment

The careful planning of KS3 English assessments into any scheme of work is crucial and, as such, a whole chapter is devoted to this particular stage of the planning cycle. Within Chapter 3, 'Assessment in Key Stage 3 English', there is a detailed exploration of the types of summative and formative assessment that have been and are currently used in this proposed KS3 English curriculum model.

Stage seven: Intervention

The penultimate stage of the planning cycle which precedes Stage One is also crucial to this proposed KS3 English curriculum model and, as such, the nature of intervention and how it is built into this proposed curriculum model are also explored in depth in Chapter 4, 'Inclusion and Challenging the Most Able in Key Stage 3 English'. Although differentiation in terms of planning has been briefly touched upon in this particular chapter, it too, like assessment, requires a great deal more investigation as to how this is encouraged within KS3 English teaching in this proposed curriculum model.

The final stage of the proposed planning cycle is the one that brings us back to its beginning: 'Stage One: KS3 English *curriculum review'*, which currently takes place over two days on an annual basis. By adopting this cyclical process that evolves, absorbs and develops over time it means that this is a robust KS3 English curriculum model that will be able to mould around any more changes that might take place at a national level. Over the past two and a half years there have been changes to the planning and delivery of different schemes of work along the way but, because the cycle is firmly embedded into the way the department works, it means that it isn't too time-consuming or arduous to make any necessary changes based on the collaborative feedback that has been received and acted on throughout the academic year.

Notes

1   *Key Stage 3: the wasted years,* Ofsted, September 2015; https://www.gov.uk/government/publications/key-stage-3-the-wasted-years.
2   Bloom, Benjamin S., Hastings, John T. and Madaus, George F., 1971. *Handbook on Formative and Summative Evaluation of Student Learning.* New York: McGraw-Hill, Inc.
3   *Statutory guidance: National curriculum in England: English programmes of study,* Department for Education, September 2013 (updated, July 2014); https://

www.gov.uk/government/publications/national-curriculum-in-england-english-programmes-of-study.

4   *A big picture of the secondary curriculum,* Qualifications and Curriculum Development Agency (updated, January 2010); http://webarchive.nationalarchives.gov.uk/20100823130703/http://curriculum.qcda.gov.uk/uploads/BigPicture_sec_05_tcm8-15743.pdf.

5   *English Programme of study for key stage 3 and attainment targets* (This is an extract from The National Curriculum 2007), Qualifications and Curriculum Authority, 2007; http://webarchive.nationalarchives.gov.uk/20100823130703/http://curriculum.qcda.gov.uk/uploads/QCA-07-3332-pEnglish3_tcm8-399.pdf.

6   Smith, Laurence and Walsh, Michael, n.d. *Let's think in English.* London: King's College, London; https://www.letsthinkinenglish.org.

7   *Key Stage Two: 2016 Assessment and reporting arrangements (ARA),* Standards & Testing Agency (updated, March 2016); https://www.gov.uk/government/uploads/system/uploads/attachment_data/file/512097/2016_KS2_Assessmentandreportingarrangements__ARA__PDFA.pdf.

8   *English - Appendix 1: Spelling, Statutory guidance: National curriculum in England: English programmes of study,* Department for Education, September 2013 (updated, July 2014); https://www.gov.uk/government/uploads/system/uploads/attachment_data/file/239784/English_Appendix_1_-_Spelling.pdf.

CHAPTER 3

Assessment in Key Stage 3 English

Tuesday, 14 October 2008, is one of those days in my career that is forever etched in my mind. Newly appointed as Head of English in a large secondary school and eleven days away from my wedding, I clearly remember sitting in the classroom looking wistfully outside at the crisp, sunny autumnal day, trying to disengage with the sheer amount of stress that was clouding my mind. Suddenly, as if a literary fairy tale was becoming reality, the Head of Religious Education came bounding over to the Head of Maths and me with a huge smile on their face before saying, 'Have you heard? The government has scrapped the KS3 SATs!' And with that statement, the cliché was complete. Looking out of the window where the sun was quite low but shining brightly, it was clear that I was experiencing the effects of pathetic fallacy firsthand.

In 1988 when attainment targets and levels were introduced with the National Curriculum, there were no KS3 English statutory assessments to accompany the new programmes of study. It was not until 1991 that the first Standard Assessments Tests (SATs) were phased in to the KS3 National Curriculum. By the early noughties, however, the SATs had taken on a life of their own and in KS3 English they became synonymous with the shorter writing task, the longer writing task, the reading paper and the close analysis of two key scenes from a Shakespeare play. Facetiously, I always thought that this final analytical task must have been something the great bard had always aspired to as a fledgling playwright.

Putting my cynicism to one side, the whole of Year 9 during those dark days was cloaked in anxiety as English teachers prepared their pupils to complete their KS3 SATs. It didn't matter how many times English departments were instructed by the National Strategies not to teach to the test, with such high stakes in terms of how a school was judged at that time, it proved impossible to steer away from teaching the Year 9 pupils how to achieve those all-important and elusive Level 5 and Level 6s in their KS3 English SATs.

Life without levels in KS3 English

The reason for this brief synopsis of the history of assessment and its tentative relationship with the KS3 English National Curriculum Programmes of Study, is because of the profound effect that this turbulent back story shares with the current policy behind assessment in KS3 English, also known as 'Life Without Levels' (LWL). Now that the shockwaves of a life without levels across the KS3 English curriculum is subsiding, I think it is also important to address 'LWSL' (Living with Sub-Levels) and how *Assessing pupils' progress*[1] (APP) became a dominant force in many KS3 English departments across England with acolytes, such as me, believing that this was a brilliant way of standardising marking.

It is also important to recognise how the advent of the National Strategies KS3 English APP contributed to the *Commission on Assessment without Levels: Final report*.[2] In the years following the prescriptive yet seminal moment when assessment was formally standardised in KS3 English through APP, it was inevitable that a growing dependency on the assessment grids would contribute to the demise of levels. Whatever the pros and cons of APP and the fine line between the sublevels that it created, for English in particular, it did bring consistency in marking to this most subjective of subjects, as it meant that KS3 English would be standardised nationally for the first time since 1988.

In the *Key Stage 3: The wasted years?* report, Ofsted inspectors record that Senior Leaders had said that, 'the removal of levels was a big challenge for them, causing uncertainty'.[3] Furthermore, the senior leaders interviewed 'were concerned that this would lead to a lack of consistency' (Ofsted: 2015). The 'uncertainty' and anxiety expressed by the senior leaders in their interviews to Ofsted inspectors demonstrates just how monolithic levels, sub-levels and a reliance on APP had become; especially for KS3 English departments across England. It is ironic, however, that the senior leaders expressed such concerns, as only twenty-eight years ago there was a 'Life Before Levels' which proves that schools can function successfully without them.

In the 'Foreword from the chair of the commission' to the *Commission on Assessment without Levels: Final report*, John McIntosh, MBE, states that it is high-quality *formative assessment* that goes to the very heart of good teaching (DFE and Standards and Testing Agency: 2015) and the report dedicates a large section to 'The Purposes and principles of assessment'. The fact that this section spans eleven pages and takes the time to remind all of the parties involved in teaching young people in England about the differences between the 'Purposes and principles' of summative and formative assessment suggests that these are either new concepts or not fully understood by the profession.

However, the importance of using formative assessment or 'formative evaluation',[4] (the term adopted by Bloom, Hastings and Madaus in 1971) to help move the pupils on with their learning in the *Commission on Assessment without Levels: Final report* is nothing new. There is a cliché in many staffrooms that 'everything comes full circle'. However, even though teachers are often perceived as being a little jaded by the many changes in education, life without levels is proof that they are always right.

In Benjamin S. Bloom, J. Thomas Hastings and George F. Madaus's, *Handbook on formative and summative evaluation of student learning* (1971), the chapter on 'Learning for mastery' summarises that the purpose of summative evaluation is when 'the teacher and student know when the instruction has been effective' and makes it clear that assessing pupils against an 'arbitrary and relative set of standards' (1971, p. 53) does not support pupil progression in terms of mastering a subject.

It is disappointing that the work of Bloom, Hastings and Madaus is not specifically referred to in the *Commission on Assessment without Levels: Final report*, especially when there is reference to the term 'Mastery' in the final report without drawing on its pedagogical origins. According to the section on "Mastery in assessment" in the 2015 report mastery learning is interpreted as:

> *A specific approach in which learning is broken down into discrete units and presented in logical order. Pupils are required to demonstrate mastery of learning from each unit before being allowed to move on to the next, with the assumption that all pupils will achieve this level of mastery if they are appropriately supported. Some may take longer and need more help, but all will get there in the end.*

> (DFE and Standards and Testing Agency: 2015)

By using words such as 'specific approach', 'discrete units' and 'logical order' there is a clinical undertone in this summation of what mastery learning is. Furthermore, the closing generalisation to this paragraph that says 'all will get there in the end' is a particular platitude that cannot be quantified or qualified.

Such descriptions, I think, detract from the positive experience of mastery learning. The use of formative assessment to help students master parts of their learning before moving on to new material is far more personalised and uplifting in the summary given by Bloom, Hastings and Madaus (1971, p. 54) when they state:

> *Frequent formative evaluation tests pace the students' learning and help motivate them to put forth the necessary effort at the proper time. The appropriate*

> *use of these tests helps ensure that each set of learning tasks has been*
> *thoroughly mastered before subsequent tasks are started.*

This above statement is far more in tune with the way that I have used formative assessment over the years and it is something that has evolved and has become more effective as each planning cycle begins.

KS3 assessment in the proposed KS3 English curriculum model

Assessment is the one area of this proposed KS3 curriculum model that has changed the most over the past two and a half years: partly influenced by changes on a national level and partly because of the evolving nature of the model itself. Initially, a number of APP tasks were incorporated into the long- and medium-term plans, as well as the sequences for learning as one of the ways of formally assessing the pupils' knowledge at the end of a scheme of work. During the first planning cycle between 2014 and 2015, these APP tasks were deemed fit for purpose as they supported teachers, especially non-specialists, in standardising their KS3 English marking. However, from the start of the planning cycle for 2016–2017 there are no APP tasks in this proposed curriculum model. Additionally, the use of the APP grids to level work in Years 8 and 9 will be phased out as the national programme of life without levels is phased in with the current Year 7.

One of the highlights of the *Commission on Assessment without Levels: Final report* is the fact that, "The Commission decided at the onset not to prescribe any particular model for in-school assessment" (DFE and Standards and Testing Agency: 2015). Initially, creating some assessment criteria for KS3 English after relying heavily on the APP speaking and listening, reading and writing grids for over ten years seemed like a daunting challenge. However, as the APP weaning process is nearly complete, there is an underlying excitement that measuring a pupil's progress is "no longer synonymous with moving on to the next level" (DFE and Standards and Testing Agency: 2015) and that the KS3 English assessment that underpins their learning is more autonomous. There is a sense of liberation outlined by the Commission in the report when they state:

> *Assessment without levels gives schools the opportunity to develop their own*
> *approaches to assessment that focus on teaching and learning and are tailored*
> *to the curriculum followed by the school.*
>
> (DFE and Standards and Testing Agency: 2015)

It is this idea of tailoring the assessment to the proposed KS3 English curriculum model that is singularly the most exciting part of the Commission's report.

Tables 3.1 and 3.2 showcase some of the proposed formats for the KS3 English assessment grids in reading. As life without levels in KS3 English began a year after it was introduced in the primary phase, alongside the teaching of the new English Language and English Literature specifications in September 2015, it meant that there was an extra twelve months in which to design a system that would link assessment between KS2 and KS4 English. In the initial stages, I was able to work with some of my colleagues from the KS3 English working group when looking at the wording of the skills descriptors that would be used. Once I had finalised the wording I presented the draft assessment sheets that I had put together to the rest of the KS3 English working group for proofreading purposes. After changing the odd modal verb, we decided to use these draft assessment sheets to standardise examples of Year 9 work at the second of the two conferences that we had arranged. Delegates who attended the conference commended these draft assessment grids. Subsequently, this positive peer feedback helped me create the final drafts that I presented to my Senior Leadership Team before they were amended even further to fit in with the whole-school KS3 assessment policy.

The most important factor for me when designing the new KS3 English assessment grids was to use visuals alongside the wording, as Tables 3.1 and 3.2 demonstrate. I have always been a visual learner and following the dyslexia training that I completed in 2011, it became extremely important that I incorporated visuals to complement the written text on all of my teaching resources; whether it was a worksheet or something to be projected to the whole class. In the 'Final report of the Commission on Assessment without Levels' there is a section dedicated to 'Ensuring a fully inclusive approach to assessment' that states:

> Assessment methods may need to be adapted for some pupils with SEN and disabilities, for example, by using visual stimuli and alternative means of communication.

> (DFE and Standards and Testing Agency: 2015)

I would go one stage further and suggest that visuals should not be used for special education needs (SEN) pupils only; rather, I propose that all KS3 English assessment criteria should have the option of incorporating visuals for it to be truly inclusive. Pupils with mild dyslexia or other specific learning difficulties may also be sat in a top set Year 8 English class without it being officially documented.

33

Table 3.1 Reading assessment grid: Silver.

	English KS3: Reading Assessment Grid: Silver	
Working	**Reading Descriptors**	**Achieved?** ✓ x 3
At Greater Depth	Relevant points clearly identified, including appropriate textual reference.	
	Comments securely based in textual evidence, with some detailed exploration of layers of meaning.	
	Some detailed explorations of how structural choices support the writer's purpose.	
	Some detailed explanations of language choices with comments on how these words impact on the reader.	
	Viewpoint clearly identified and explained through close analysis of the text, with clear explanation of the effect on the reader.	
	Some explorations of how contexts affect meaning.	
At the Expected Standard	Most relevant points clearly identified and supported, included those selected from different points in the text.	
	Comments develop an explanation of inferred meaning based on textual detail.	
	Comments on structural choices show a general awareness of the author's craft, with an identification of organisation at text level, including form.	
	Various features of writer's use of language identified, with some explanation of the effect.	
	Main purpose and viewpoint clearly identified through overview and some explanation, including the effect on the reader.	
	Identifies similarities and differences between texts with some explanation, including how contexts contribute to meaning.	
Towards the Expected Standard	Some relevant points identified and supported by generally appropriate textual reference or quotation.	
	Comments make inference based on evidence from different points in the text.	
	Some basic features of organisation at text level identified.	
	Simple comments on writers' language choices made.	
	Main purpose identified with simple comments on the writer's viewpoint and the effect on the reader.	
	Features of similar texts identified with simple comments made about the effect of the writer's context.	

Table 3.2 Reading assessment grid: Developing – competent.

English KS3: Reading Assessment Grid: Developing - Competent		
Type of Learner	**Reading Descriptors**	**Achieved?** ✓ x 3
Emergent	Most relevant points clearly identified and supported, included those selected from different points in the text.	
	Comments develop an explanation of inferred meaning based on textual detail.	
	Comments on structural choices show a general awareness of the author's craft, with an identification of organisation at text level, including form.	
	Various features of writer's use of language identified, with some explanation of the effect.	
	Main purpose and viewpoint clearly identified through over-view and some explanation, including the effect on the reader.	
	Identifies similarities and differences between texts with some explanation, including how contexts contribute to meaning.	
Increasing	Some relevant points identified and supported by generally appropriate textual reference or quotation.	
	Comments make inference based on evidence from different points in the text.	
	Some basic features of organisation at text level identified.	
	Simple comments on writers' language choices made.	
	Main purpose identified with simple comments on the writer's viewpoint and the effect on the reader.	
	Features of similar texts identified with simple comments made about the effect of the writer's context.	
Budding	Range of strategies used to read with fluency, understanding and expression.	
	Simple points identified with some references to text.	
	Inference based on single points in a text with a mainly literal understanding.	
	Basic features of organisation at text level identified.	
	Basic features of writer's language identified.	
	Comments identify main purpose and express a personal reference.	
	Simple connections made between texts with some recognition of context.	

Bloom, Hastings and Madaus (1971, p. 45), in their opening to the chapter 'Learning for Mastery', state 'that our students vary in many ways can never be forgotten'. It was not until the completion of my dyslexia training in 2011 that the idea of preparing lessons that accommodate all learning styles became firmly entrenched in my daily planning. The training gave me the self-awareness to realise that I would tend to veer towards one learning style in my teaching at the expense of the others. In 'Learning for Mastery', Bloom, Hastings and Madaus continue this point about personalised learning by saying that 'one may start with the very different assumption that individual students may need very different types and quality of instruction to achieve mastery' (1971, p. 47). The nature of tailoring lessons, resources and assessments to individual styles is regularly reviewed in the KS3 English planning cycle.

Whilst visuals on assessment grids like those in Tables 3.1 and 3.2 are a very simple way of creating some variety to what can otherwise be quite a disaffecting experience for a number of KS3 English pupils, at least it helps to break down the sheer amount of writing in an aesthetic way. Since 2005 I have written a number of APP pupil-speak grids and, unfortunately, distributed them to lots of other KS3 English teachers. At the time I genuinely believed that I was empowering KS3 English pupils by giving them the criteria that they would need for progression in a language that they understood. In retrospect, I was giving them three sheets of paper covered in words that couldn't be decoded as they held no real meaning for the pupils. Using visuals to break down the process of moving forward in learning is one way in which potentially all pupils become engaged with the KS3 English assessment process. Visuals such as images, colours and shapes are accessible to all and can have lots of underlying meaning.

I designed the small images with an illustrator on Tables 3.1 and 3.2 to visually represent each stage of progression for the pupils. In the case of Table 3.1, I sub-divided this visual even further to fit a bronze, silver and gold format so that the progression from KS2 to KS3 was even clearer for the new Year 7 cohort, as *Towards the Expected Standard, At the Expected Standard* and *At Greater Depth* would be terms that the pupils would be familiar with from their Year 6 teacher assessments.[5] Additionally, the idea of issuing a bronze, silver and gold award once the pupils had mastered their designated assessment stage was built on the success of the KS3 pupils' response to the bronze, silver and gold spelling awards that was implemented in September 2015. Having something tangible to collect in assembly in front of their peers has proved to be popular and contributed to the rise in the pupils' spelling ages. (See Chapter 6: 'LAC and SPAG: Divisive or Cohesive Abbreviations in the KS3 English Curriculum?' for further details concerning the spelling awards.)

The one major feature that Tables 3.1 and 3.2 share is the fact that the pupils have to demonstrate that they are able to complete a certain skill at least three times in all areas of the criteria for them to be able to move on to the next stage of learning. Unlike levels and the APP criteria that 'used a "best-fit" model which meant that a pupil could have serious gaps in their knowledge and understanding but still be placed within the level' (DFE and Standards and Testing Agency: 2015), these examples of assessment criteria in Tables 3.1 and 3.2 only recognised mastery in a pupil's learning once it has been confirmed that the pupil has completed the skill at least three times. The evidence for this mastery of a particular skill can come from either the formative marking of the pupil's exercise book or from a formalised end-of-term assessment.

Moderation in the proposed KS3 English curriculum model

Other significant changes that have occurred over the last two planning cycles with regard to assessment is that the number of formalised end-of-term assessments has significantly decreased. Between 2014 and 2015 pupils were expected to cover one speaking and listening, one reading and one writing formalised assessment per term in Years 7, 8 and 9. In 2015–2016 this was reduced to two assessments per term and finally between 2016 and 2017 this has been whittled down to one formalised assessment per year group, per term. In those initial stages of the planning cycle, I was still in an APP state of mind whereby I fell into the trap of teaching becoming 'focused on getting pupils across the next threshold instead of ensuring they were secure in the knowledge and understanding defined in the programmes of study' (DFE and Standards and Testing Agency: 2015). Plus, the amount of marking that the number and frequency of these assessments presented the department with was unsustainable.

The assessment arrangements for 2016–2017 are far more manageable and, more importantly, purposeful; this will be the first year in this proposed KS3 English curriculum model where the assessments will take place using a carousel system. For example, in the autumn term, Year 7 pupils will complete a formalised speaking and listening assessment, Year 8 will complete a formalised writing assessment and Year 9 will complete a formalised reading assessment. This will rotate around for the spring term and finally, the summer term, until all pupils in Years 7, 8 and 9 will have completed one formalised assessment in each of the skills in KS3 English. All of these assessments are clearly marked on the long- and medium-term plans and the sequences of learning.

These formalised assessments are an important part of this proposed KS3 English curriculum as they provide the periodic summative information that helps 'the teacher and student know whether the instruction has been effective' (Bloom, Hastings and Madaus: p. 52). Nevertheless, by reducing the number of formalised assessments, it means that there can be more focus on supporting the pupils help master the crucial skills of speaking and listening, reading and writing in KS3 English.

The importance of moderating the pupil's work in this proposed KS3 English curriculum model has evolved rather than been changed or omitted over the past three planning cycles. A concern raised in the *Key Stage 3: The wasted years?* report was that 'just over a quarter of senior leaders spoken to said that they conducted internal moderation during Key Stage Three' (Ofsted: 2015). The importance of standardising work through departmental dialogue in the earliest stages of the proposed KS3 English curriculum model cannot be underestimated. Not only does it support non-specialists or members of the department who are less familiar with assessment in KS3 English, it creates consistency in marking for all members of the department.

During the first planning cycle, there was no specific guidance on the process of internal moderation in the proposed KS3 English model. By the second planning cycle between 2015 to 2016 that guidance was put in place but deemed too onerous, especially as there was a high number of formally assessed tasks that needed completing. Table 3.3 and Figure 3.1 outline the internal moderation process that takes place during this current third planning cycle.

Table 3.3 outlines the process of moderation. Swapping three scripts, as outlined in the process in Table 3.3, is not only more manageable but also purposeful. Accompanying the process is the KS3 English moderation pro forma sheet that records the discussions and decisions that have been made. Although this is to officially document final summative decisions about a piece of work, it is the formative evaluation section at the bottom of Table 3.3 that proves the most useful part of the process. The section that is entitled 'Formative Evaluation: Teaching and Learning Outcomes and Actions' is the part of the moderation process that is the most powerful as it feeds back to the rest of the department to help improve their own teaching and, more importantly, increase pupils' learning outcomes.

There are two further areas of development that need to be considered over the next learning cycle in terms of moving on the process of moderation in this proposed KS3 English curriculum model. The first is to develop 'external moderation with other schools to ensure the accuracy of assessment' (Ofsted: 2015). When designing the life without levels criteria, being given the opportunity to standardise work with other KS3 English colleagues across Suffolk was an extremely powerful and useful experience. Unfortunately, because of logistics, this has not happened since the opportunity to facilitate such meetings is more

Table 3.3 Moderation process.

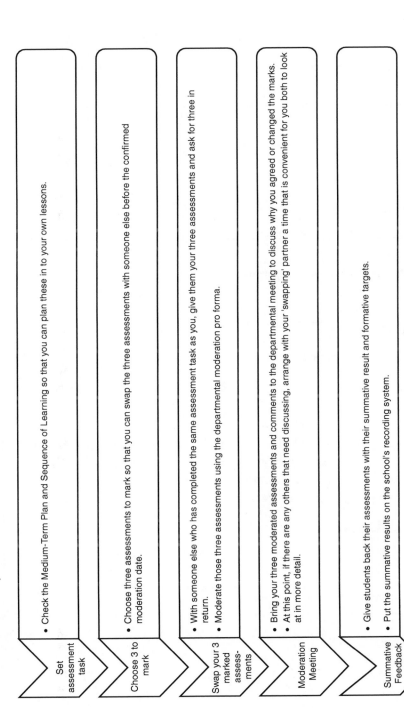

Set assessment task	• Check the Medium-Term Plan and Sequence of Learning so that you can plan these in to your own lessons.
Choose 3 to mark	• Choose three assessments to mark so that you can swap the three assessments with someone else before the confirmed moderation date.
Swap your 3 marked assessments	• With someone else who has completed the same assessment task as you, give them your three assessments and ask for three in return. • Moderate those three assessments using the departmental moderation pro forma.
Moderation Meeting	• Bring your three moderated assessments and comments to the departmental meeting to discuss why you agreed or changed the marks. • At this point, if there are any others that need discussing, arrange with your 'swapping' partner a time that is convenient for you both to look at in more detail.
Summative Feedback	• Give students back their assessments with their summative result and formative targets. • Put the summative results on the school's recording system.

Teacher's Name:	
Moderated by:	
Due date for moderated script:	

Unit:	Student:
Task:	End of KS3 Target:

Summative Moderation

Level/Grade Awarded:	Agreed? Yes / No

Reason(s) to justify confirmation/adjustment

Formative Evaluation: Teaching and Learning Outcomes and Actions

Figure 3.1 Example moderation pro forma sheet.

difficult in this current educational climate. Nevertheless, external moderation of tasks between the KS3 English department and their feeder primary schools is also beneficial and far more straightforward to organise as well, and this is hoped to take place during the next planning cycle.

More formalised moderation of the KS3 English exercise books may also take place during the next planning cycle, as this is currently an informal yet extremely useful exercise that occurs on an ad hoc basis. During such moderation, teachers would complete the section that is entitled 'Formative Evaluation: Teaching and Learning Outcomes and Actions' on Table 3.3. By doing this, the department can disseminate the moderation of exercise books in a formalised way without it becoming burdensome and they can ascertain how well the department as a whole is fulfilling the principle, as stated by Bloom, Hastings and Madaus (1971, p. 54), that 'The diagnosis should be accompanied by a very specific prescription if the students are to do anything about it'. Formalising a review of the formative assessment that teachers give their students in their exercise books is an opportunity to log good practice and share with others; especially those who are non-specialist English teachers, part-time or newly qualified, as it provides an up-to-date checklist of what is working in terms of moving pupils on with their learning within the department.

Examination-style questions in the proposed KS3 English curriculum model

As someone who was forced to start their GCSE English Language and English Literature courses in Year 9 to help the school reach their targets back in the early 1990s, the thought of pupils losing out on one year of their statutory right to a three-year KS3 English curriculum is a factor that fuels my passion behind this proposed curriculum model. Indeed, Ofsted's *Moving English Forward* report dedicated a section to 'An inappropriate emphasis on tests and examinations'.[6]

Figure 3.2 demonstrates the typical assessment tasks in stage five of the learning cycle (Assessing 1. Knowledge and 2. Skills) found on a medium term at the front of a scheme of work. These short, differentiated tasks help the teacher to ascertain whether a pupil has mastered the skills and knowledge that they have been presented with during the unit and whether further work is needed via intervention. Unfortunately, due to the pressures of the new GCSE English Language and English Literature specifications, which are closed book and not differentiated, the decision has been made during this planning cycle that certain schemes of work will have specific KS4 exam-style questions on GCSE texts in stage five of the learning cycle on the medium-term plan. This

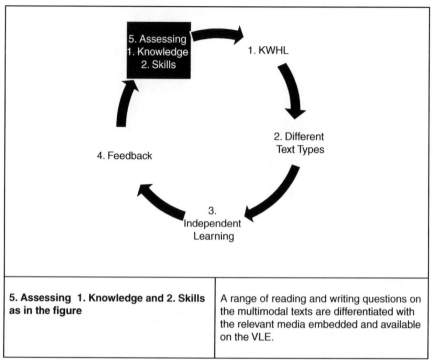

5. Assessing 1. Knowledge and 2. Skills as in the figure	A range of reading and writing questions on the multimodal texts are differentiated with the relevant media embedded and available on the VLE.

Figure 3.2 Stage 5 assessment tasks.

will ensure that the pupils are provided with the earliest opportunities to prac-tise these formulaic skills.

This was not an easy decision to make. However, for those pupils who have an inefficient working memory like mine, it was decided that they would need to familiarise themselves with the way that they will be questioned in their GCSE at the earliest opportunity. It is hoped that by doing this it will avert the inevitable shock that pupils face when they see these texts and questions for the first time in Year 10. This decision also contributes to this book's central premise that a robust and well-prepared KS3 English curriculum should stop a school's resources being diverted into the inevitable firefighting in the sum-mer term of Year 11. Ultimately, the overarching goal for Bloom, Hastings and Madaus's principle to 'formative evaluation' is that (1971, p. 56):

> When the student has mastered a subject and when he receives both objective and subjective indications of this, there are profound changes in his view of himself and of the outer world.

This holistic approach to moving pupils' learning forward underpins this proposed KS3 English curriculum model with the goal for the student being that

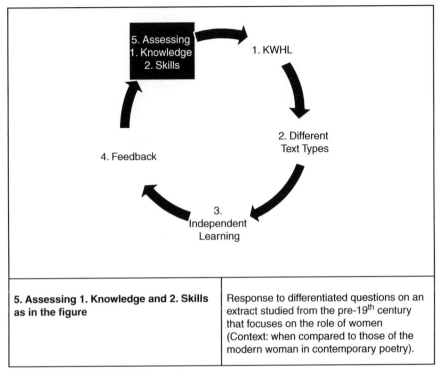

| **5. Assessing 1. Knowledge and 2. Skills as in the figure** | Response to differentiated questions on an extract studied from the pre-19th century that focuses on the role of women (Context: when compared to those of the modern woman in contemporary poetry). |

Figure 3.3 Stage 5 assessment tasks.

'He begins to "like" it and want more of it' (Bloom, Hastings and Madaus: 1971, p. 56). If it means this self-recognition and confidence must start in Year 7 so that a pupil feels that they can respond to closed-book and non-differentiated questions and tiers in their final GCSE exams, then difficult decisions like those outlined in Figure 3.3 must happen to prepare the pupils.

What happens, though, when there are the inevitable changes in KS3 English assessment at national level? If talk in staffrooms across the country is correct and educational policy does indeed come full circle, will that mean levels and sublevels or their equivalent being reintroduced into the National Curriculum in England? Even more horrifying, will the KS3 English SATs or something similar emerge from the KS3 assessment abyss? Only if an English department is allocated the time to regularly review their KS3 curriculum on an annual or biannual basis will teachers be prepared for the next major shift in KS3 English assessment on a national level. In the interim, frequent evaluation during and at the end of each planning cycle is paramount to the KS3 English curriculum's success. Being given the time for reflection about the appropriateness and purposefulness of the departmental assessment policy is crucial if the pupils are to progress with their learning in any proposed KS3 English curriculum model.

Notes

1 *Assessing pupils' progress (APP) in English*, Department for Children, Schools and Families, August 2008; http://webarchive.nationalarchives. gov.uk/20110113104120/http://nationalstrategies.standards.dcsf.gov.uk/ node/16051?uc=force_uj.

2 *Commission on Assessment Without Levels: Final report*, Department for Education and Standards and Testing Agency, 17 September 2015; https://www. gov.uk/government/publications/commission-on-assessment-without-levels-final-report.

3 *Key Stage 3: The wasted years?*, Ofsted, September 2015; https://www.gov.uk/ government/publications/key-stage-3-the-wasted-years.

4 Bloom, Benjamin S., Hastings, J. Thomas and Madaus, George F., 1971. *Handbook on Formative and Summative Evaluation of Student Learning.* New York: McGraw-Hill, Inc.

5 *Key stage 2 teacher assessment*, Standards and Testing Agency, 12 September 2016; https://www.gov.uk/government/collections/key-stage-2-teacher-assessment.

6 *Moving English Forward: Action to raise standards in English*, Ofsted, April 2013; https://www.gov.uk/government/publications/moving-english-forward.

Inclusion and challenging the most able in Key Stage 3 English

Creating a KS3 English curriculum model that supports weaker pupils and challenges their more able peers is simultaneously the most difficult and time-consuming part of the planning cycle outlined in Chapter 2. It is also the most worthwhile and productive investment of time if it means that the summative outcomes for Years 7, 8 and 9 are successful in terms of all KS3 English pupils making the required level of progress by the end of the academic year. Before a new KS3 English departmental review starts, candid discussion is needed as to whether the schemes of work, their differentiated learning objectives and any subsequent intervention strategies have had a positive impact on the pupils' achievement during the previous planning cycle.

One way into this conversation is by focusing on those KS3 pupils who were identified as underachieving at the beginning of the academic year and measuring their level of progress over the three terms. Using data seems a clinical starting point in which to measure the success of the year's KS3 English planning cycle. However, if the success of a school solely relies on its numerical outcomes, then this is the best way to start to begin the evaluation of the proposed KS3 English curriculum model.

All pupils must be given the best possible chance from an early stage in their secondary education to achieve their potential by the end of KS4. If this means that the KS3 English curriculum needs to adapt and evolve during the next planning cycle, then this is the stage that reviews the success of the differentiation and intervention that has been put in place. Subsequently, this will start the initial decision-making process about the future of the existing schemes of work in the proposed KS3 English curriculum model.

Extra time has also been spent at different stages of the planning cycle throughout the year, targeted at the more frequent evaluation of the success of the differentiation employed within individual schemes of work. Although this is a laborious task, it is the words of Bloom, Hastings and Madaus in the chapter on 'Learning for Mastery' from their *Handbook on Formative and Summative Evalu-*

ation of Student Learning[1] that continue to resonate and inspire the reasons as to why this regular reflection is necessary, when they state (1971: p. 50):

> *Whatever the amount of time allowed by the school and the curriculum for particular subjects or learning tasks, it is likely to be too much for some students and not enough for others.*

By collating information that measures the success of differentiation and intervention in schemes of work at regular points throughout the planning cycle, it helps to supplement any major decisions about what will evolve, change or be omitted from the proposed KS3 English curriculum model during the next academic year.

One of the central aims in the book is to provide a range of examples of how differentiation is implemented at various stages in a scheme of work. In this chapter, however, I am seeking to demonstrate how differentiation is generically threaded through all stages of planning using the key language of 'Support' and 'Challenge'. Additionally, I will look at how different levels of learning objectives and learning outcomes contribute to the inclusive nature of this KS3 English curriculum model that I am proposing. These learning objectives and outcomes serve as a constant reminder to all teachers that one size does not fit all; even when KS3 English classes are grouped per the pupils' competency, there is still a range of abilities that need to be accommodated within any lesson. Likewise, another important strand underpinning this proposed KS3 English curriculum model is the fact that it serves to support and inform the teachers who are non-specialists, as well as Higher Learning Teaching Assistants (HLTAs), about the best ways to implement differentiation in any KS3 English or intervention lessons that they will deliver.

Inclusion and challenge in medium-term planning

'Support' and 'Challenge' as signposts for teachers in medium-term planning

Although there is reference to differentiated schemes of work and assessments on the long-term plan for this proposed KS3 English curriculum model, it is the medium-term plan where the class teacher first sees the variety of differentiating learning tools that are available to use in the proceeding sequence of learning. These are summarised to help pupils of all abilities strive towards mastering up to all three parts of the 'Success Criteria' that can also be found on the medium-term plan.

Bloom, Hastings and Madaus state in 'Learning for Mastery' (1971, p. 47):

One may start with the very different assumption that individual students may need very different types and qualities of instruction to achieve mastery.

Table 4.1 is a close-up of the different types and qualities of instruction from a medium-term plan. All the medium-term plans in this proposed KS3 English curriculum model have this 'Support' and 'Challenge' section as demonstrated in Table 4.1 to inform the teachers of the various levels of differentiation that need to be addressed with examples of how the teachers might want to implement this support and challenge in their lessons. Generic advice in the 'Support' part of the differentiation section about font type, size and colour is found in every single medium-term plan, as are references to resources such as writing frames that are used to support pupils scaffold their written work.

Once again, there is general advice provided in the 'Challenge' part of the differentiation section in Table 4.1 that appears in all the medium-term plans,

Table 4.1

An example of differentiation on a Medium-Term Plan	
Support	*All paper resources to be on cream/light blue paper with a minimum of 12+ Comic Sans/Arial font-type and all projected resources to be on a cream/light blue background with Comic Sans/Arial font-type set at a minimum of 28+ with fewer words and symbols/images to support key words, terms and ideas for those pupils who experience a barrier to reading written texts. *Guided and independent reading using fiction and non-fiction cue cards: Focus on word level, working up to sentence level questions and tasks in guided reading groups. Even within the lower sets, the pupils will be grouped according to ability with colour-coded tasks to support differentiation. *The provision of writing frames in extended writing tasks. *Adopting roles in speaking and listening tasks that students feel confident with. *Socratic dialogue to boost confidence in formal group discussion as the pupils are there to support each other. Although the teacher may choose a straight forward class debate arrangement to encourage discussion as this is a more familiar discursive set-up. *Active reading strategies to help the pupils engage with unseen texts. *There is an alternative scheme of work available in this unit that is specifically designed to help pupils consolidate what they have learned at a steady pace. However, pupils will also be able to access a whole range of differentiated resources within the main sequence of learning as well. *The reading assessment is clearly structured with prompts and focuses on the close analysis **of one poem**.
Challenge	* Guided and independent reading using fiction and non-fiction cue cards: pupils to focus on sentence and text level questions and tasks. **Choice and Challenge:** Pupils to independently choose from a number of colour-coded guided questions and activities from across the range of guided and independent reading fiction and non-fiction cue cards. *Pupils will have the option to choose from a range of challenge activities in lessons and for homework. *Pupils will be grouped for guided reading and writing tasks according to their confidence and ability; however, there will be a great deal of focus on independent learning during sustained pieces of writing. *The reading assessment has few prompts and asks to compare two poems in detail. *All pupils are encouraged to vary their roles in Socratic discussion to develop their speaking and listening skills.

such as: *'Pupils will have the option to choose from a range of challenge activities in lessons and for homework.'* Teachers must look closely at the sequences of learning to see where there the suggested resources and activities are, but it is felt important to draw their attention to their availability in the short-term plan.

Other generic advice that can be found in the 'Support' and 'Challenge' section in all the medium-term plans in this proposed KS3 English curriculum model is the reference to resources available to support guided and independent reading. Three years ago, whilst cross-sitting between two schools, I designed packs of colour-coded fiction and non-fiction cue cards that were readily differentiated and easy to manoeuvre between two schools. These cue cards have now been given to individual teachers to support differentiation in the questioning of fiction and non-fiction texts.

The medium-term plans in this proposed KS3 English curriculum model direct the teachers towards these cue cards so they know that they have them at their disposal daily. Examples of how these cue cards are differentiated can be seen in Table 4.1. For example, in the 'Support' section, pupils will focus on questions at word level and build up to questions that focus on sentence level. Whereas in the 'Challenge' section, teachers are advised to use either sentence or text-level questioning depending on the level of challenge that they want to present to the individual members in their class.

In the 'Support' and 'Challenge' section of a medium-term plan, there is also advice that is not generic and specific to that scheme of work. For example, in Table 4.1 there is reference to the formal assessment that the pupils will write. For the less able pupils, they will focus on the close analysis of one of the poems studied and the teacher's short-term planning should account for this; whereas, the more able pupils will be challenged with comparing two very difficult poems and, likewise, the teacher also needs to prepare for this high level of challenge in their short-term planning.

'Inclusion' and 'Challenge' in a sequence of learning

'Support' and 'Challenge' as signposts for teachers in a sequence of learning

Table 4.2 demonstrates how a range of suggested ideas and activities may help a teacher plan for differentiation within their class. As the sequences of learning are reviewed at the end of each planning cycle based on how successful they have been during the previous academic year, the content in the second and third columns can often change per the collaborative feedback given by the department. As ever, it is the mandatory differentiated learning objectives that

Table 4.2

Week	Learning Objectives	Suggested Resources to help fulfil the Week's Learning Objectives	Suggested Homework
4	1) To **identify** the main arguments in the home-school debate **(Low Level Skill)** 2) To **develop** these ideas about the home-school debate and **organise** them into arguments and counter-arguments **(Mid-Level Skills)** 3) To **appraise** the ideas of others and **justify** our responses about the home-school debate during a Socratic discussion **(High Level Skills)**	• To read chapters 11 – 23 of the novel (Audiobook option on the *Staff Shared Network* area) • Shared reading followed by guided reading activities (**Support:** Yellow for characterisation with increasing challenge across abilities to **Challenge:** grey for structure and blue for hooks) • **Speaking and Listening:** *Socratic Discussion:* Question: *Why do parents choose to educate their children at home?* (**Support:** Debate: *Which do you think is the best idea: learning at home or learning at school? Can you give at least three reasons why?*) Resources for the speaking and listening tasks can be found on the *Staff Shared Network* area. *Further guidance on organising a Socratic discussion can be found on the *Staff Shared Network* area where you can also watch the departmental training video: *How to organise a Socratic discussion*	**Scheme of Work Homework Project (Week 4):** William Blake (**Challenge!** And The Romantics) Writing to Inform; Explain; Describe (See homework project sheet for exact details). **Further Challenge** To create a list of 10 questions that you would like to ask the novella's female protagonist. Next, choose the best 5 questions from your list and justify your reasons for choosing them.

must be met and it is entirely up to the teacher how they wish to get their pupils to master those skills.

The sequence of learning as exemplified in Table 4.2 takes on board the advice given by Bloom, Hastings and Madaus (1971, p. 49) in 'Learning for Mastery' when it says: 'It is that each type of material may serve as a means of helping individual students at selected points in the learning process.' There is a great deal of content and coverage suggested on the sequence of learning in Table 4.2 to help the pupils master the skills outlined in the mandatory learning objectives. However, the second and third columns are 'suggested' and it is up to the class teacher as to whether they use these ideas and materials. The class teacher understands the pupils they teach better than the designer of the KS3 English curriculum model. Often they have their own ideas and resources that can be personalised for the individual needs of pupils in their class and are often much better suited than those that are suggested in the sequence of learning.

Small group intervention and how it should complement a KS3 English scheme of work

Another benefit of having clearly differentiated learning objectives in a sequence of learning is the help and support that it can provide to those teachers, higher level teaching assistants (HLTAs) and teaching assistants (TAs) who deliver small group intervention. In 'Learning for Mastery' it states that:

> In our own experience we have found that small groups (two or three students) meeting regularly to go over points of difficulty in the learning process were most effective.
>
> (Bloom, Hastings and Madaus: 1971, p. 48)

Providing those professionals who deliver small group intervention with a clear scheme of work that demonstrates how differentiated learning objectives and outcomes can be mastered will meaningfully supplement the vital work that happens in those small group sessions. It creates a point of dialogue between the class teacher and the teacher, HLTA or TA so that the intervention that takes place can be much more targeted.

Sharing the learning objectives and suggested tasks on the schemes of work with the teacher, HLTA or TA means that these small group sessions are not arbitrary because they are feeding into something much broader. Consequently, by instigating this dialogue between the class teacher and the professional who will deliver the intervention, these supplementary lessons fit in to a much wider context and support the pupil's mastery of the skills and knowledge that are outlined in the scheme of work.

Unfortunately, most of the small group intervention strategies that take place in schools across England are aimed at less able pupils who are not secondary school ready or not making the required levels of progress in English. Therefore, in this proposed KS3 English curriculum model I have aspired to make sure that the level of support and challenge is equal across all stages of planning and ensure that it reflects the observation made by Ofsted in the *Moving English Forward* report that:

> there are good opportunities now for teachers to be more flexible in their approach to teaching and planning lessons. This should include a greater readiness to respond to the unexpected in lessons and to change the direction of lessons as they develop.[2]

The sequence of learning in a scheme of work is not designed to be prescriptive and dictate that the level of support or challenge must be delivered in a certain way. As Table 4.2 demonstrates, the suggested 'Support' and 'Challenge' resources, activities and homework on a sequence of learning are simply put in place to remind English teachers that this proposed KS3 English curriculum is inclusive yet must be flexible as well.

Balancing the needs of *all* pupils in KS3 English

Challenging the most able KS3 English pupils in any potential curriculum model is often overlooked because of the level of support and intervention that is targeted at those pupils who are less able. Astonishingly, in the 2015 *Key Stage 3: The wasted years?* report it stated that:

> About two thirds of the senior leaders interviewed for this Key Stage 3 survey talked about how they met the needs of low-ability pupils, particularly to help them to make progress with literacy. However, only one in 10 focused on how the most able could make the best possible progress.[3]

I do not believe that the level of support that less able pupils and those with Specific Learning Difficulties (SPLD) receive should diminish and be alternatively re-directed to challenging the most able. As a mum to a young child who has SPLD and who will more than likely be given an Educational Health Care Plan (EHCP) in the not-so distant future for a speech and language disorder, I would be horrified to think that any level of support that he, or others like him, may receive would be reduced so that time and resources would be focused instead into challenging the most able. Rather, I am suggesting that there needs to be a much more holistic approach to any potential KS3 English curriculum model; it needs to be egalitarian in the way it addresses the needs of the most and least able whilst challenging all of the pupils who fall somewhere in between the two.

Even though this proposed KS3 English curriculum is at the beginning of its third planning cycle, the rigour and challenge has always commenced at the beginning of Year 7. It is important that all pupils feel from an early stage that KS3 English matters and they will need to push themselves to meet the varying levels of challenges that they will be presented with. For example, throughout Year 7, the most able pupils are issued with difficult poems and unseen texts, as well as being issued with the completed version of a pre-nineteenth-century text when compared to the shorter, more manageable extracts aimed at the less able. The values of a challenging curriculum are at the heart of this proposed KS3 English curriculum model. In the suggested resources and homework columns on a sequence of learning all pupils, especially the most able, are often asked to complete tasks that are unfamiliar to them and leave them outside of their comfort zone.

In Ofsted's March 2015 report, *The most able students: An update on progress since June 2013*, not only did inspectors observe that there is a '[l]ack of challenge at the start of Key Stage 3',[4] they also stated that:

> *In the most effective schools inspectors visited, the curriculum at Key Stage 3 was carefully structured, taking into account the most able students' knowledge and understanding. In these schools, leaders knew that, for the most able, knowledge and understanding of content was vitally important alongside the development of resilience and knowing how to conduct their own research.*
>
> (Ofsted: 2015)

In Ofsted's report, it is clear that the schools who have made advances in tailoring their curriculum to challenging their most able pupils have done so at KS4 at the expense of KS3. This belief that getting things in place at KS4 such as challenging the most able is frustrating; this challenge should begin at the very start of Year 7 to avoid the inevitable firefighting in the summer term before the Year 11s complete their English Language and English Literature examinations.

As the planning cycles continue over the coming years, this proposed KS3 English curriculum model will strive to be as inclusive, rigorous and challenging as it was when it was first introduced in September 2014. Ultimately, getting pupils of all abilities to become resilient and independent learners is at the very heart of this proposed KS3 English curriculum model. At all stages of planning it seeks to balance the needs of all pupils in Years 7, 8 and 9 whilst giving them the confidence to master the knowledge and skills outlined in the schemes of work, so that they challenge themselves to exceed and succeed in KS3 English.

Notes

1   Bloom, Benjamin S., Hastings, John T. and Madaus, George F., 1971. *Handbook on Formative and Summative Evaluation of Student Learning*. New York: McGraw-Hill, Inc.
2   *Moving English forward: Action to raise standards in English*, Ofsted, April 2013; https://www.gov.uk/government/publications/moving-english-forward.
3   *Key Stage 3: the wasted years?*, Ofsted, September 2015; https://www.gov.uk/government/publications/key-stage-3-the-wasted-years.
4   *The most able students: an update on progress since June 2013*, Ofsted, March 2015; https://www.gov.uk/government/publications/the-most-able-students-an-update-on-progress-since-june-2013.

CHAPTER 5

Planning for English transition across the primary and secondary phase

Even though, as a secondary school teacher, I have delivered countless Year 7 taster English lessons to Year 6 pupils in the summer term before their secondary education begins, it was not until I taught, and subsequently became Head of English in a middle school, that I finally appreciated the importance of the transition from the primary phase to the secondary phase of a pupil's education. During the three years that I taught Years 5 to 8, I saw at first hand how moving from the English primary curriculum to the English secondary curriculum was more than a simple transitional phase from one key stage to another. In the middle school, planning the English KS3 curriculum flowed naturally from Year 6 to Year 7 as the pupils built on their subject knowledge and developed their study skills.

As a trainee teacher in secondary schools and readily supplied with the National Literacy Strategy for bedtime reading, I was ignorant of the Year 6 pupils' already extensive knowledge and often felt that I was teaching the eager eleven- to twelve-year-old pupils sitting in front of me features of English as if it was radically new material that they had never had access to before they came to my lessons. In those early stages of my career, it rarely occurred to me that many of the Year 7 pupils that I was teaching had already successfully learned these components in their primary schools. For example, one Year 7 unit I designed was called *An Introduction to Shakespeare's World*, and a sea of bemused faces looked at me when I was teaching the wonders of the Globe theatre and the antics of its groundlings to my new pupils. It later transpired that many of those sitting in my classroom had already been introduced to Shakespeare's world in KS2 and, as such, this unit of work had to be adapted so that it could build on the pupils' prior knowledge, whilst also catering for those in Year 6 who, for whatever reason, had not been introduced to Shakespeare in their primary schools.

I have used the plural 'schools' here because therein lies the main logistical difference between the transition from the primary to the secondary curriculum in a middle school when compared to its two-tiered counterparts. The simple reason that the planning between Year 6 and Year 7 was seamless and more successful in a middle school was because all the pupils who were transitioning from the primary to the secondary English curriculum were often in the same building and therefore the department could use this to their advantage in its planning. However, in some cases, there are often many feeder primary schools from different localities and different demographics that feed into a secondary school. For example, in rural and coastal areas there can be as many as nineteen primary schools from which the pupils feed into a secondary school. The question of how to accommodate all the English curriculum transition needs on a logistical and practical level when considering the large number of primary schools involved is one that continues to challenge me as I try to bridge the two phases in the KS3 English curriculum model that I am proposing.

Nevertheless, aside from my acknowledgement of these significantly different logistical arrangements, my three-year tenure in the middle school helped me to fully appreciate how transition in the two-tier system had to become more than the annual Year 6 to 7 English transition project that was dusted down and shared between the secondary school and its feeder primaries. For example, a piece of free writing as part of an English transition unit completed at the end of Year 6 shows a Year 7 English teacher some insight into what type of writer their new pupil might be, but it doesn't tell the teacher what type of learner they are.

There have also been times during my career in the two-tiered system when Year 7 pupils study specific poems, *novels* and other forms of texts that they have already either referred to or completed in their primary schools. This issue of repeating material in English is acknowledged in the *Key Stage 3: The wasted years?*[1] report as a 'particular concern', because if work has already been covered by pupils in their primary schools and is then repeated in their secondary school, it means that those particular Year 7 pupils are not challenged with new material. Where possible, the English transition project needs to work alongside cross-phase long-term planning with as many of the feeder primary schools involved as possible. By doing this, Year 6 pupils feel a sense of continuity from the beginning of Year 7 when they begin their new secondary English curriculum. As part of the continuing self-reflection and evaluation process that takes place throughout the KS3 English planning cycle, the question of building in KS2 English planning successfully is frequently addressed

54

throughout the academic year during English primary liaison meetings with the main feeder primary schools.

Primary transition in *Key Stage 3: The wasted years?*

Two sections of the *Key Stage 3: the wasted years?* report is dedicated to the findings that (1) 'Cross-phase partnerships with primary schools are crucial' and (2) 'Many secondary schools do not build sufficiently on pupils' prior learning' (Ofsted: 2015). It is noted in the findings of the first section cited that 'In 13 out of 14 schools visited, there was evidence of effective work between the two phases. Where they worked closely, the results were powerful'. In terms of the latter, the report states: 'The issue of repeating the same work was of particular concern ... For English, this figure was 29%.' Furthermore, the case studies[2] offered to support the findings of these statements have reaffirmed my original belief gained from my middle school teaching experience that carefully built-in cross-phase planning working alongside creative transition projects is crucial to the success of bridging the primary and secondary English curricula.

Ofsted's September 2015 report was generic and focused on the whole of KS3; therefore it looked at transition between KS2 and KS3 across a range of subjects, as well as commenting on pastoral transition between Years 6 and 7. However, the earlier 2012 Ofsted report, *Moving English forward*, which had spearheaded the KS3 English working party that I became part of, goes into more detail about the issues that surround 'Transition from Key Stage Two to Key Stage Three'[3] in English. Not only does the report provide more specific reasons behind the decline of cross-phase transition in English than the *Key Stage 3: The wasted years?* report, it also bullet-points quite clearly a range of 'effective individual activities' that were 'noted during the survey' (Ofsted: 2012). This broad range of activities can be used and adapted in most cross-phase English transition situations whether the schools are in urban, rural or coastal areas.

This notion of adaptability certainly struck a chord as, in my experience, one size does not fit all and the different types of primary schools that may feed into the secondary school need to be able to mould any English transition projects that they are given according to the size and ability of the Year 6 cohort that they teach. If several of the cohort are going to different schools, it is essential that a meaningful and successful English primary transition project is implemented, especially for the pupils going to the secondary school where the transitional work has been set. However, the project also needs to accommodate the Year 6 teacher too as, in my experience, they can have up to half a dozen transition projects to deliver and return to the several different secondary schools that their pupils are going to.

Equally important is this idea of adaptability and evolution in terms of planning across the two phases into any KS3 English curriculum model that the secondary school adopts. At this point it is worth reiterating that the planning cycle outlined in Chapter 2 helps support the department as it prompts teachers to continuously reflect and evaluate whether certain features of the KS3 English curriculum model, such as the cross-phase English transition project, are working in terms of meeting the department's success criteria for that year.

Evaluation of the cross-phase English primary transition project

With regard to evaluating the success of the cross-phase English primary transition project, this reflective discussion must involve the feeder primary school English teachers. There must be a willingness from secondary teachers to adapt and change the English transition project, and subsequently, any long-term planning, according to the feedback given from primary colleagues. Essentially, as both *Key Stage 3: The wasted years?* and *Moving English on* suggest, a positive relationship between the Year 6 English teachers and their secondary colleagues is at the centre of strengthening cross-phase relationships and English is a subject which can prompt a great deal of creativity in the bridge between Year 6 and Year 7.

After observing Year 6 pupils in an English lesson and looking closely at the 2014 English National Curriculum programmes of study across the primary and secondary phase, it is clear that there is one common denominator across the whole national curriculum and, in particular, in English. The 'English appendix 1: Spelling'[4] and 'English appendix 2: Vocabulary, grammar and punctuation' are statutory documents (although the middle and right-hand columns in appendix 1 are non-statutory guidance) and can be used as the basis of a creative transitional project that will fit most primary demographics and localities and, consequently, be easily embedded into KS3 English long-term planning.

The creative use of a cross-phase project based on spelling, vocabulary, grammar and punctuation that is easily differentiated, enjoyable and not onerous for the Year 6 teacher to facilitate could provide the transitional bedrock needed for English long-term planning between Key Stages Two and Three. Such a project not only bridges the primary and secondary phase in English seamlessly, it is also extremely informative for Year 7 English teachers in terms of planning for the year ahead. For example, ascertaining the pupils' previous level of understanding of spelling, vocabulary, grammar and punctuation in KS2 without simply relying on their final SATs score means that the Year 7 English teacher can plan lessons that will ensure pupils can secure this knowledge of the mechanics of English during their first year of secondary education.

Proposed cross-phase English transitional project

What's in a word?

As a result of discussions with Year 6 English teachers, the *What's in a word?* project is etymology based and is designed to be fun, engaging and not arduous following the Year 6 SATs and writing teaching assessments. The introductory lesson is led by a secondary school English teacher using their school's lesson plan. This is shared with the Year 6 teacher so that they become increasingly familiar with how lessons are delivered when their pupils begin Year 7. The introductory lesson's expected learning outcomes outline how pupils will consolidate what they have already learned in KS2 in terms of word derivation and spelling rules whilst also working towards their secure understanding of these rules in Year 7. The Year 6 pupils will also be able to familiarise themselves with elements of the secondary school's autumn 1 long-term plan for Year 7 as well as beginning to understand how the secondary school's marking policy works.

Even though the secondary school will provide the one or two words that the Year 6 pupils will be expected to investigate, the *What's in a word?* template is completely flexible and pupils can engage with as many headings as they want, or as many as the Year 6 teacher thinks is appropriate for their class, especially if they only have one or two pupils feeding into the secondary school. It might be that the class teacher decides to let an extremely able pupil tackle many, if not all, of the headings. Alternatively, the Year 6 teacher may decide to encourage their pupils to do one or two headings well and present their findings in an engaging way. At all times, the secondary English department is aware that at this point it is the Year 6 English teacher who fully understands the requirements of their pupils and that is why there is a great deal of flexibility throughout the proposed transitional *What's in a word?* project to cater for as many needs as possible – especially if many feeder primary schools are involved.

The headings on the *What's in a word?* template range from simple investigative tasks such as '*Does this word have any homophones or homographs?*' to more creative pieces of writing that require self-assessment and possible re-drafting. For example, '*Can you write a poem or a descriptive piece of writing with the key word as its subject?*' The Year 6 pupils are expected to research the designated words at home or school whilst being encouraged to use other subjects such as technology or art and design to present their findings creatively.

Alternatively, the Year 6 teacher may decide to issue the blank *What's in a word?* pro forma provided by the secondary school English department, which can then be modified per the needs of their class. Ultimately, one size does not fit all and, following discussions with Year 6 English teachers, there needs to be a certain degree of flexibility so that they can accommodate the needs of *all* pupils whether they are feeding into several different secondary schools or not.

Assessment of the proposed *What's in a word?* cross-phase English transitional project

A mandatory requirement of the proposed *What's in a word?* English transitional project is that upon its completion the Year 6 teacher works through the first two sections of the peer/self/teacher assessment template. This is because the template has been adapted to reflect the high school's marking policy and allows the Year 6 pupils to familiarise themselves with how their work will be assessed once they begin Year 7. Subsequently, Year 6 will complete the peer and self-assessment area of the template and finally, in early July, the pupils' projects and the partially completed assessment template are given to their Year 7 English teachers so that the teacher assessment column can be completed. The assessment template should not be too arduous for the pupils and teacher but it should (a) help the Year 6 pupils familiarise themselves with the way their work will be marked at KS3 and (b) let the Year 7 teacher feedback on the project as a whole. For example, as well as assessing how well their new pupils understand etymology and the mechanics of English, the teacher can comment on the pupils' creativity and ability to put a research-based project together. Ultimately, the Year 7 teacher will be able to gauge from the project and the self- and peer-assessment template what type of learner they can expect in the classroom when they begin the KS3 English curriculum in autumn 1.

This project is in its infancy and, as part of the ongoing reflection and feedback which is at the heart of the KS3 English planning cycle, the *What's in a word?* proposed cross-phase transitional project may be adapted or even changed depending on (a) feedback from Year 6 teachers and (b) the quality of the work that the Year 7 teachers receive from their new pupils. This type of research project that is being proposed is creative, informative and should accommodate a number of logistical and practical needs. However, if subsequent discussions with Year 6 English teachers in the autumn term reveal that the project needs amending or changing then ultimately, as part of the pedagogy at the heart of the KS3 English planning cycle, there needs to be an acceptance and agreement from the feeder primary schools and the secondary school that the transitional project should be amended or even changed completely.

Building a transitional project into KS3 English long-term planning

Whatever is the outcome of these discussions concerning how successful the *What's in a word?* project has been, I still believe that using 'English appendix 1: Spelling'[5] and 'English appendix 2: Vocabulary, grammar and punctuation' as the common denominator that links the primary English and secondary English curricula together is the most straightforward way of initiating a transitional project that also incorporates cross-phase planning.

As Table 5.1 shows, in the autumn term, there is a different approach to the teaching of spelling, punctuation and grammar (SPAG) in Year 7 when compared to Years 8 and 9. Although I will be looking at SPAG in more detail in Chapter 6, I wanted to use Table 5.1 to demonstrate how the transition project can feed into the Year 7 long-term plan and be used as a learning tool that can be referred to in the weekly spelling, punctuation and grammar lessons. If the *What's in a word?* English transition project is successful, then the Year 7 English teachers can use the headings as a starting point in these weekly lessons. However, if it is not, I would strongly advise the use of SPAG as an accessible starting point in English cross-phase planning. Even if there are many primary schools involved, the majority of the Year 6 pupils should be able to bring their prior knowledge of spelling, punctuation and grammar to the secondary school and be familiar with the material that they are presented with as they begin their Year 7 English lessons.

Primary transition: Next steps

Cross-phase transition projects aside, there are a number of other steps that need to be taken in terms of primary transition when considering the next KS3 planning cycle. At the top of the list is looking at KS2 planning from as many feeder primary schools as possible and subsequently auditing the texts that are read and studied in Years 3 to 6. By doing this, the secondary English department can be confident that they will not repeat texts and material meaning that all Year 7 pupils can be challenged as they are presented with texts that they have not studied before.

Table 5.1 Long-term plan: Spelling, punctuation and grammar.

Key Stage Three English: 2016-2017: Autumn Two		
Year 7	Year 8	Year 9
Words, Sounds, Images	*Words, Sounds, Images*	Library Lesson: Year 9 Class Reader **Guided Reading Activities (Differentiated)**

Library Lesson: Year 9 Class Reader
Guided Reading Activities (Differentiated)

Year 9

Words, Sounds, Images
Secure knowledge of the different approaches to seen and unseen poetry (4 weeks+3Weeks A1)

Unit Name: *Why War?*
(Text Types: Multi-Modal, Still Images, Report, Recount, Biography, Propaganda, Speech, WW1 Poetry, Timelines, Letters, Commentary)

Cauldron of Characterisation
Secure knowledge and perceptive analysis of Conan-Doyle's Famous Detective (pre and post 20th-century character evaluations of the representation of Sherlock Holmes) (3Weeks)

Unit Name: *It's All Elementary!* **(Text Types: Multi-Modal, Still Images, Differentiated Prose, Biography, Newspaper Reports)**

SPAG Lesson: Fortnightly (A2): Sp: Consolidation and secure knowledge of complex syllabic and irregular spelt words **P:** Consolidation and Secure knowledge of punctuation as well as using sophisticated punctuation techniques for effect in writing. **G:** Ensuring secure use of sentence variety to create certain effects in writing.

Assessment Tasks for Autumn 2
Reading: *Comparing and Contrasting values in the poetry of the First World War* (See Sequence of Learning for differentiated tasks)

GCSE Assessment Objectives Covered: Language: Writing: Paper 2: Writing to Inform/Explain (AO5 and AO6) **Reading:** Close Analysis of Language/Structure (AO2) **Literature:** Contextual Poetry Comparison (AO2 and AO3)

PLTS: Let's Think in English Lesson: *The Last Days of Okawa* Reasoning pattern: Narrative Sequencing

---

Library Lesson: Year 8 Class Reader:
Guided Reading Activities (Differentiated)

Year 8

Words, Sounds, Images
Revision and progression upon the different approaches to seen and unseen poetry (3 Weeks+3Weeks A1)

Unit Name: *Questioning the Voice in Contemporary Poetry* **(Text Types: Post-Modern Poetry. Multi-Modal, Still Images, Recount, Commentary, Autobiography)**

Cauldron of Characterisation
Analysis of a range of different characters across a range of short stories by Roald Dahl (4 Weeks)

Unit Name: *Being a Detective!* **(Text Types: Short Stories, Multi-Modal, Still Images, Biography, Newspaper Reports)**

SPAG Lesson: Fortnightly (A2): Sp: Securing knowledge of complex polysyllabic words by focusing on prefixes and suffixes (*Challenge:* Spelling Challenge and Preparatory Spelling Bee List) **P:** Ensuring Accuracy and Variety **G:** Revising the appropriateness of syntax in formal and informal texts.

Assessment Tasks for Autumn 2
Writing: *Write the opening paragraphs for a detective story* (See Sequence of Learning for differentiated task)

GCSE Assessment Objectives Covered: Language: Writing: Paper 1: Imaginary Writing (AO5/AO6) **Reading:** Close Analysis of Language and Structure (AO2) **Literature:** Poetry Comparison (AO1 and AO2)

PLTS: Let's Think in English Lesson: *The Open Window:* Reasoning pattern: Narrative Sequencing

---

Library Lesson: Year 7 Group Readers:
Guided Reading Activities (Differentiated)

Year 7

Revision of Poetry Across Time: Medieval to the Victorians (4 Weeks + 3Weeks A1)

Unit Name: *Shaking Up the Senses!* **(Text Types: Multi-Modal, Still Images, Pop Music Lyrics, Different Types of Poems)**

Cauldron of Characterisation
Revision of the differences between direct and indirect characterisation with close attention to the language of Dickens (3 Weeks)

Unit Name: *Will the real Scrooge Please stand up?* **(Text Types: Multi-Modal, Still Images, Differentiated Prose, Script, Biography)**

SPAG Lesson: Weekly (A2) Sp: To Consolidate and Secure our knowledge of Year 3 – 6 Spelling Lists (*Challenge:* Spelling Challenge and Preparatory Spelling Bee List) **P:** To revise different methods to avoid comma splicing **G:** To secure our understanding of: Relative clauses; Modal Verbs and Adverbs; Adverbials **(SEN:** Secure understanding of subject-verb-object)

Assessment Tasks for Autumn 2:
Speaking and Listening:
Group Performance of a Ballad

GCSE Assessment Objectives Covered: Language: Writing: Paper 1: Imaginary Writing (AO5) **Reading:** Close Analysis of Language and Structure (AO2)

PLTS: Let's Think in English Lesson: *Jabberwocky* Reasoning Pattern: Classification **(Withdrawn from the LTE Programme. As such, will change in 2017 review)**

Christmas Holidays

Often, the Year 6 to Year 7 pupils are the most excited and eager cohort in the school as they are at the start of a new learning journey. It is the responsibility of all involved with cross-phase English transition to hone in on this willingness to absorb brand new material. Additionally, it is up to English teachers from the primary and secondary phase to give the pupils the confidence to reflect and build on their prior learning as they move from Year 6 to Year 7. Ultimately, successful primary transition to the secondary school can only be achieved through supportive collaboration between KS2 and KS3 English teachers and a willingness to adapt or even change any existing arrangements if they are not deemed suitable or appropriate for a Year 6 cohort.

Notes

1 *Key Stage 3: The wasted years?*, Ofsted, September 2015; https://www.gov.uk/government/publications/key-stage-3-the-wasted-years.
2 *Ofsted key stage 3 curriculum survey 2015: 8 good practice case studies*, Ofsted, September 2015; https://www.gov.uk/government/publications/ofsted-key-stage-3-curriculum-survey-2015-8-good-practice-case-studies.
3 *Moving English forward: Action to raise standards in English*, Ofsted, April 2013; https://www.gov.uk/government/publications/moving-english-forward.
4 *Statutory guidance: National curriculum in England: English programmes of study*, Department for Education, September (updated, July 2014); https://www.gov.uk/government/publications/national-curriculum-in-england-english-programmes-of-study.
5 *Statutory guidance: National curriculum in England: English programmes of study*, Department for Education, September (updated, July 2014); https://www.gov.uk/government/publications/national-curriculum-in-england-english-programmes-of-study.

LAC and SPAG: Divisive or cohesive abbreviations in the KS3 English curriculum?

Many allegations about lower standards today come from employers, who maintain that young people joining them from school cannot write grammatically, are poor spellers, and generally express themselves badly.[1]

The Bullock Report (1975), *A language for life*

In the forty-two years since Sir Alan Bullock and an independent committee were commissioned by Edward Heath's government to write a report that looked at the way English language was taught in schools, the ensuing debate surrounding the importance of literacy across the curriculum (LAC), and who is responsible for overseeing and delivering it, continues. There is no one solution that seems to satisfy these two respective problems. Consecutive governments have tried raising standards in reading and writing in schools across England. Yet, by the 2012 *Moving English forward* report, which was produced nearly forty years after the seminal *A language for life* was first published, Ofsted reported that even though the LAC debate had been 'long established',[2] unfortunately, 'efforts to raise literacy as a whole-school initiative have tended at best to have a short-term impact'. Puns aside, this *lack of LAC* longevity is deeply concerning, especially as all subjects now have accountability for the pupils' sound understanding of spelling, punctuation and grammar (more affectionately known across schools in England as SPAG) across KS4.

In my previous chapter concerning English cross-phase transition, I suggested that using 'English appendix 1: Spelling'[3] and 'English appendix 2: Vocabulary, grammar and punctuation' was the most straightforward, common denominator that links the primary English and secondary English curriculums together. In this chapter I will develop this idea one step further. As well as showing how the teaching of SPAG is implemented into the proposed KS3 English curriculum, I will also address the importance of how other subjects across KS3 need to become an active part of the planning cycle in the future if literacy skills such as SPAG are to be successfully transferred across the curriculum. Ultimately, the statement made by Ofsted in the opening to its *Moving English forward* report says, 'There can be no more important subject than English in the school's curriculum' (Ofsted: April 2013) and this needs to be heeded by all subjects at KS3. All teachers are accountable for helping pupils consolidate and build on the skills that they learn in English.

Implementing SPAG into a KS3 English model

The departmental review that took place during the first planning cycle between 2014 and 2015 focused on how successful the schemes of work, different texts and assessments had been in this new KS3 English curriculum model. During that first review it was decided that between 2015 and 2016 the focus would be on SPAG. This decision was taken as the schemes of work, texts and assessments that had been introduced the previous year were efficaciously embedding themselves into the new proposed KS3 English curriculum. Therefore, it was felt that the next priority was to ensure that the department was ready for the drastic changes to the rigorous SPAG element of the KS2 SATs. Having sat the KS2 SPAG test myself alongside other secondary English teachers, it was clear that the SPAG provision in the 2014–2015 KS3 English planning cycle would not appropriately consolidate the pupils' learning and, therefore, it needed to be developed accordingly so that it too would become successfully embedded into the proposed KS3 English curriculum model.

Using the 'English appendix 1: Spelling' and 'English appendix 2: Vocabulary, grammar and punctuation' as a starting point, I decided to conduct a departmental audit to see exactly who understood and could apply the terminology listed in these documents. This was a useful exercise, most notably for *me*, as it made me realise that there were elements of the extensive lists that I needed to revise. More importantly, it helped get an overarching view as to where all of the English teachers, specialist and non-specialists, were in terms of their ability to understand a SPAG term and apply it. With regard to English subject specialism, in *A language for life* (1975, p. 9) it states:

> The attitude still prevails that most teachers can turn their hand to it *[English]*
> *without appropriate initial qualifications or additional training. In our view*
> *such an attitude is based on an ignorance of the demands of English teaching*
> *and the knowledge required of its practitioners.*

In a perfect world, all secondary pupils would be taught by specialist English teachers. However, until shortages in specialist teachers are addressed nationally and the desired utopia outlined by Bullock and his colleagues back in 1975 is realised, departments will have to continue to support, in all areas of the subject, the non-specialists and HLTAs who deliver secondary English lessons.

The audit provided a clear overview of where the department's strengths and areas for development were and who might be able to provide peer support in helping others strengthen their subject knowledge. It also helped to support the cross-phase transition between primary and secondary English because the Year 7 teachers were able to see exactly what the Year 6 pupils were expected to have covered with regard to SPAG (which is pretty much everything there is to know about spelling, punctuation and grammar!), so they could build on this prior learning.

It was decided that within the vast sphere that SPAG covers, spelling and the reinforcement of spelling rules would be the foundation for the new SPAG strategy between 2015 and 2016. The whole premise of the KS3 English planning cycle is centred on regular evaluation. However, another important part of the cycle is making sure that certain elements of the KS3 English programmes of study are embedded successfully, as opposed to trying to introduce several new fleeting concepts at once. Spelling, it was decided, would be the most straightforward of the SPAG constituents to be implemented into the 2015–2016 planning cycle and so this became our focus. From a retrospective point of view, this has proved to be an extremely successful decision because there is a great deal more energy and confidence in the delivery of SPAG lessons as the department begins the 2016–2017 planning cycle.

Two of the main features of the spelling programme included were the introduction of bronze, silver and gold spelling awards across KS3, which meant weekly spelling tests to be undertaken by all pupils like those they would have experienced in their primary schools and also, as part of the end of year English competitions, an inaugural school spelling bee for the Year 8 pupils took place in the summer term. The spelling bee was differentiated so that all Year 8 pupils could potentially take part in the grand final in July. Creating a competitive element in the KS3 spelling programme proved very popular amongst the pupils and there was a buzz around the Years 7, 8 and 9 assemblies when pupils received their bronze, silver and gold awards in front of their peers. Likewise, the Year 8s were excited to compete to be part of the form team that would take part in the spelling bee. In the spelling tests taken every six months by KS3 pupils, there was a clear increase in the number of months added to their spelling age when compared to the results of the tests taken in the 2014–2015 planning cycle.

Table 6.1 Example of mandatory SPAG learning outcomes from the Autumn 1 and 2 long-term and medium-term plans (2016 – 2017).

SPAG learning outcomes from the Autumn 1 and 2 long-term and medium-term plans (2016 – 2017)		
Year 7	Year 8	Year 9
SPAG Lesson: Weekly (A2) Sp: To Consolidate and Secure our knowledge of Year 3 – 6 Spelling Lists (***Challenge:*** Spelling Challenge and Preparatory Spelling Bee List) **P:** To revise different methods to avoid comma splicing **G:** To secure our understanding of: Relative clauses; Modal Verbs and Adverbs; Adverbials (**SEN:** Secure understanding of subject-verb-object)	**SPAG Lesson: Fortnightly (A2): Sp:** Securing knowledge of complex polysyllabic words by focusing on prefixes and suffixes (***Challenge:*** Spelling Challenge and Preparatory Spelling Bee List) **P:** Ensuring Accuracy and Variety **G:** Revising the appropriateness of syntax in formal and informal texts.	**SPAG Lesson: Fortnightly (A2): Sp:** Consolidation and secure knowledge of complex syllabic and irregular spelt words **P:** Consolidation and Secure knowledge of punctuation as well as using sophisticated punctuation techniques for effect in writing. **G:** Ensuring secure use of sentence variety to create certain effects in writing.

Following on from the success of the spelling programme introduced in the 2015–2016 planning cycle, the other pieces of the SPAG puzzle also needed to fit into this proposed KS3 English curriculum model with the incorporation of the formalised teaching of punctuation, grammar and vocabulary. Up until and including the planning cycle from 2015 to 2016, it specified on the KS3 long-term plans that SPAG lessons were to take place fortnightly. However, as Table 6.1 demonstrates, at the beginning of this planning cycle for 2016–2017, it was decided that mandatory SPAG lessons are to take place weekly for Year 7 but remain fortnightly for Year 8 and Year 9.

As the current Year 7 become Year 8 in September 2017 they will continue with weekly SPAG lessons that adopt the starter-middle-plenary format and will follow weekly lesson plans for spelling, punctuation, grammar and vocabulary until they finish Year 9 at the end of 2019. By this time, the pupils will work on practising, consolidating and securing their entire SPAG knowledge until they begin the challenging GCSE specifications in Year 10. Teaching discrete, weekly SPAG lessons is not a new concept in the secondary phase. During my career it is something that I have always done. However, making it mandatory on the long- and medium-term plans on the proposed KS3 English curriculum model means that it formalises SPAG as a strategy for the whole department; this continuity from Year 7 to Year 9 will benefit all staff and pupils. Having observed the way literacy lessons are delivered at primary schools over the years has reaffirmed my belief that this is the best way to teach spelling, punctuation, grammar and vocabulary as it is a familiar format for all Year 7s, no matter which school that they have come from.

The rationale behind the weekly Year 7 SPAG lessons for 2016 to 2017 is simply to strive to make sure that all of the Year 7 pupils are at their 'expected' level in writing by the summer term. After their long summer break, the key-words in the Year 7 learning outcomes for SPAG (see Table 6.1) are 'revise' and 'consolidate'. The Year 6 pupils who took the SATs in the summer of 2016 only experienced two years of the Primary National Curriculum, so it is likely that there will be gaps in their SPAG knowledge that need addressing.

Nevertheless, after observing Year 6 lessons, this particular cohort is more likely to have a greater grasp on the mechanics of English than their Years 8 and 9 counterparts. In this period of transition from the old curriculum to the new, it is more a case of trying a number of strategies to make sure that all of the Year 7s are confident with SPAG in their main English lesson when studying the texts outlined in stage two of the scheme of work. The termly KS3 English staff evaluations during 2016–2017 will focus specifically on the effectiveness of the SPAG rationale to ascertain what elements need to be adapted or changed. This is a brave new world and with statutory elements such as English appendix 1 and appendix 2 in it, there is an opportunity to create a successful transition between the primary and secondary phases.

However, during 2016–2017, the current Year 7 pupils will not complete the spelling tests that provide the teacher with a spelling age until they begin Year 8. Rather, they will work on revising and consolidating their knowledge of the statutory Years 3 to 4 and Years 5 to 6 spelling lists (DFE: 2014) so that those who are not secondary school ready, have the best possible chance to achieve the expected level in writing at the end of Year 7. I have called the Years 3 to 4 'Spelling List A: Pupil Checklist' (see Table 6.2) and the Years 5–6 'Spelling List B: Pupil Checklist' so as not to make the pupils feel like they are regressing.

As the pupils will have practised these spellings extensively in their primary schools it means that these words are already familiar to them and they all have a greater chance of succeeding. As we are in the new(ish) world of mastery outlined in Chapter 3, the checklists (see Table 6.2) need to see evidence of the pupils spelling these words correctly three times so that Year 7 teachers can confidently say that their pupils have mastered these particular spellings. Furthermore, as Table 6.1 demonstrates, those pupils who complete both spelling lists A and B will be challenged to begin the bronze, silver and gold spelling awards, in addition to being issued with the preparatory spelling bee list.

The regular testing of 'Spelling List A: Pupil Checklist' and 'Spelling List B: Pupil Checklist' forms part of the starter-middle-plenary SPAG lesson plan that the Year 7 teachers will follow. Although this National Strategy-style approach

Table 6.2 Spelling checklist.

Name:				Year 7 English Teacher:			
Spelling List A.	✓	✓	✓	**Spelling List A.**	✓	✓	✓
accident(ally)				knowledge			
actual(ly)				learn			
address				length			
answer				library			
appear				material			
arrive				medicine			
believe				mention			
bicycle				minute			
breath				natural			
breathe				naughty			
build				notice			
busy/business				occasion(ally)			
calendar				often			
caught				opposite			
centre				ordinary			
century				particular			
certain				peculiar			
circle				perhaps			
complete				popular			
consider				position			
continue				possess(ion)			
decide				possible			
describe				potatoes			
different				pressure			
difficult				probably			
disappear				promise			
early				purpose			
earth				quarter			
eight/eighth				question			
enough				recent			
exercise				regular			
experience				reign			
experiment				remember			
extreme				sentence			
famous				special			
favourite				straight			
February				strange			
forward(s)				strength			
fruit				suppose			
grammar				surprise			
group				therefore			
guard				though/although			

Table 6.2 (Continued).

Spelling List A.	✓	✓	✓	Spelling List A.	✓	✓	✓
guide				thought			
heard				through			
heart				various			
height				weight			
history				woman/women			
imagine				**Final Summary**			
increase				Date Spelling Test A was mastered:			
important							
interest							
island							

Table 6.3 Example spelling, punctuation and grammar lesson.

Arrangements for Year 7 SPAG: 2016 – 2017: Autumn Term	
SPAG Lesson: Weekly (Autumn Term Outcomes) Sp: To Consolidate and Secure our knowledge of Year 3 – 6 Spelling Lists (***Challenge:*** Spelling Challenge and Preparatory Spelling Bee List) **P:** To revise different methods to avoid comma splicing **G:** To secure our understanding of: Relative clauses; Modal Verbs and Adverbs; Adverbials (**SEN:** Secure knowledge of subject-verb-object)	
Suggested Format of a Year 7 SPAG Lesson	
Starter	• Writer's Toolkit resources (Found on the staff network) • Comma Splicing Resources (Found on the staff network)
Main	**Work through the following lesson plans:** 1. Main Clauses (S-V-O: **SEN only**) 2. Relative Pronouns and Relative Clauses 3. Modal Verbs and Adverbs 4. Adverbial Phrases All of these lessons are organised and available in their folders on the staff network. At the end of a series of lessons, there are test questions and teacher answers so that it can be ascertained as to whether the pupils are ready to move on to the next section. If they are not, then use the tests to check for common gaps in the pupils' knowledge and go over the rules again – ***Mastery not Content!***
Plenary	Spelling Test and Peer Assessment
Suggested SPAG Weekly Homework	Spelling Test Revision (**SEN: 10 Words through to the most able 30+ Words**)

is formulaic, it makes it very clear to the teacher as to what the pupils are expected to cover during the autumn term.

The added benefit of having discrete lesson plans that follow the starter-middle-plenary format (see Table 6.3) means that it helps those in the department who are non-specialist English teachers or those who come in to cover a long-term absence as they are prescriptive in their approach and support teachers who may not be as confident with SPAG as their specialist English teacher counterparts. The SPAG programme that is beginning to embed itself into this proposed KS3 English curriculum means that all Year 7 pupils have the opportunity to either fill in the gaps in their knowledge or secure and consolidate their understanding of spelling, punctuation and grammar rules. For those pupils who are not recognised as secondary school ready in English, it is at the discretion of the class teacher as to whether they want to increase the number of SPAG lessons in the autumn term so that those pupils have a better chance of catching up with their peers by the end of Year 7.

Building cohesive relationships with other departments

What happens, though, once the pupils master a spelling rule or successfully respond to a non-fiction text in an English lesson? It is likely that the moment they leave the English classroom, the majority of pupils have mentally closed the door on those particular rules or texts and moved on, in their heads, to their next lesson.

It is the problem of pupil compartmentalisation that causes the most frustration for secondary English teachers, as the young people who leave their classroom would more than likely be able to practise their English skills in their next lesson if they were reminded. In my experience, young people, especially teenagers, become sidetracked in the five-minute walk from the English classroom to the science laboratory, for example. Peer issues, the realisation that they have no dinner money and even needing the toilet during that physical five-minute movement often means that the active reading skills or grammar rules that the English teacher has painstakingly planned and delivered in their preceding lesson have been forgotten; unless, that is, the science teacher in the following lesson picks up the English baton and carries it forward. Ultimately, as *A Language for life* and *Moving English forward* and all of the LAC reports published in between 1975 and 2013 have stated, it is the responsibility of all departments to work cohesively together in order to raise standards in English.

The transference of English skills to other subject areas is not a new concept for the Year 7 pupils: in their primary schools they are taught by one or two teachers who specialise in many subjects, including English. It is the physical changes and movement at secondary school which causes problems, as the pupils' learning is disrupted because of the logistics of their new environment. Often, it is in Year 7 when this compartmentalisation of the pupils' English lessons begins and they don't necessarily make the connection between their English lesson and their following geography lesson, for example. In 1975, *A Language for life* (1975, p. 11) prophetically reported:

69

It is obvious that as society becomes more complex and makes higher demands in awareness and understanding of its members the criteria of literacy will rise.

It is vital, therefore, that all subject areas work together cohesively and are invested in any proposed KS3 English curriculum model so that they can find opportunities within their own subjects to help pupils transfer these crucial English skills learned in Year 7 and raise standards in literacy.

There are many ways in which speaking and listening, reading and writing skills can be transferred successfully across the KS3 secondary curriculum. There are lots of innovative programmes adopted by secondary schools that are proven to stop the pupils compartmentalising their learning and transferring their English skills to other parts of the curriculum. One example of how literacy across the curriculum has inserted itself into the KS3 English curriculum that I am proposing is through the schemes of work. For example, the opening lesson to the Year 7 poetry scheme of work, *Shaking up the senses!*, in autumn 1 suggests that teachers begin with the picture shown in Figure 6.1.

Alongside the picture, the Year 7 pupils are asked to consider the following questions:

- Where have you seen this display in school?
- How do the senses help us describe certain things in this subject?
- Why do you think we are showing you this display at the beginning of an English lesson?

This display is an exciting way to start a scheme of work that focuses on sensory writing in Year 7 English and shows an immediate visual connection between English and food technology. Working closely with the food technology teacher means that a positive cohesion has formed between the two subjects. The teacher, Alice Martin, has worked tirelessly to support the pupils' literacy skills in her subject. For example, I annotated recipes using the

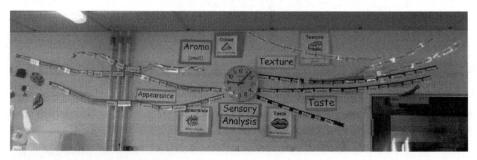

Figure 6.1 Shaking up the senses display.

terminology associated with writing to inform, describe and explain. Likewise, Alice started a breakfast club where pupils who were not secondary ready were encouraged to build on their knowledge of nutrition whilst revising and practising spelling rules and patterns.

A further example of showcasing the proposed KS3 English curriculum model to other departments in order to cohesively bring us all together, is through continual professional development (CPD). This is the second school in which I have delivered *cross-curricular* training on active reading strategies specifically designed for non-English specialists. This has proved to be successful, as the pupils can transfer the skills of skimming and scanning in an active way whereby every young person in the classroom is engaged with reading a non-fiction text which is similar to those that they would read in another subject area. This means that where there is reference to active reading strategies in the medium-term plan or in the 'Suggested Resources to help fulfil the Week's Learning Objectives' column on the sequence of learning, English teachers know that these active approaches to reading are also being practised in other curriculum areas.

SPAG and LAC working together cohesively

As the *Moving English on* report highlighted, such examples will only have a 'short term impact' (Ofsted: 2013) if they are not embedded across the school's curriculum. When I was Head of English in a middle school I led a whole-school writing project between 2006 and 2007 in a middle school. This year-long process taught me that focusing on improving literacy in one area over a period of time meant that successful and cohesive relationships could be built across the curriculum. Even before SPAG was firmly placed at the epicentre of the current KS3 English Programmes of Study, the focus of this LAC project was specifically on writing and raising standards in spelling, punctuation, vocabulary and grammar across the curriculum. In a middle school that meant raising standards in writing across the primary and secondary phase as well.

After scrutinising a wide range of writing types from across the curriculum, in May 2006 I shared the following two central findings with all staff in a CPD (Continuing Professional Development) session that I delivered:

- Conflicting marking – comments suggest a piece of work is well written when it is not (e.g. examples of poor sentence structure overlooked).
- Limited reference to the English skills to be used in extended pieces of writing.

71

As such, a list of priorities was given to the staff during that CPD session in May 2006 that would mark the start of the year-long whole-school writing project which was to begin in the following September. The priorities were:

- To ensure that teachers and teaching assistants understood why literacy across the curriculum is a whole-school priority.
- To build the confidence of non-English specialists and show how fun and accessible English can be.
- To help all those involved in the project understand that communication, whether oral or written, is at the heart of the pupils' classroom learning.
- To support pupils when they produce an extended piece of writing, particularly in Years 7 and 8.
- To demonstrate how the English department uses the standardised Assessing Pupil Progress[4] (APP) writing grids when assessing a piece of extended writing.
- To set specific whole-school writing targets each half-term.

That was a difficult CPD session to deliver as there was an inevitable element of hostility to the fact that improving writing was the responsibility of all teachers when colleagues already had a list of their own priorities within their own subject area. To allay any further anxieties and fears about this writing project being a bolt-on to their other work, I offered to support colleagues with the accurate marking of a pupil's written work by delivering lessons and finally by looking at the long-, medium- and short-term planning of other subjects to see if there were any specific opportunities which could directly refer to the writing project. I also issued a literacy departmental handbook to each curriculum area. I had designed this handbook so that it would include a series of tasks suited to non-fiction texts in addition to spelling, punctuation, vocabulary and grammar tasks that would support non-specialists. By offering this support and empathising with the anxieties of colleagues, the start of the twelve-month cohesive relationship was built.

One of the first and most notable things to go on the walls in every classroom around the school were the literacy boards as shown in Figure 6.2. Immediately, the pupils would see a number of strategies used in English to help support them with their writing, which meant that they were able to transfer these skills as they moved around the school. These boards also helped remind the class teachers what the writing targets were for each year group during that particular half-term, so it gave them a specific focus when they marked their pupils' written work.

Another example of how I worked on building a cohesive relationship with the other departments during the writing project was by delivering a Year 8

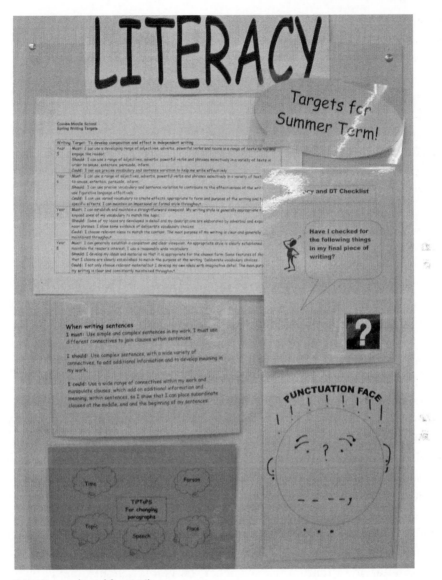

Figure 6.2 Literacy board for pupils.

resistant materials lesson whilst being observed by the class teacher (fortunately for the pupils, I was not demonstrating how to design and build the desired product, as I have no expertise in this field!). The resistant materials teacher approached me and asked if I would deliver the lesson on how to write an evaluation about the process that led to the designing of the final product. It was a daunting prospect, but well worth the planning and the effort for the resistant materials teacher, me and most importantly, the Year 8 pupils. It showed them that the structuring of an evaluative piece of writing was the same in every subject area. I reinforced the message to the pupils that they were no longer to compartmentalise evaluative writing when they leave the English classroom.

After twelve months I delivered the findings of the writing project to the rest of the school, in September 2007. To begin the CPD session, I showed them an uplifting film that I had produced which encapsulated the buzz around the writing project during 2006–2007. These included interviews with non-English teachers in the school. Their responses were extremely positive. Comments such as:

1) *'Yeah … I've got a much better knowledge … as a result of Liz's inset which was really inspiring.'* (Head of science)
2) *'I'm re-writing schemes of work … so I've been able to put in … learning Objectives specific to Literacy.'* (Head of science)
3) *'I'm looking forward to working more closely with the English department in developing some new, revised schemes of work for ICT.'* (Head of information and communications technology [ICT])
4) *'We've already agreed that the ICT lessons will produce some of the non-narrative writing assessments.'* (Head of ICT)

were extremely helpful because they came from the point of view of teachers from different subjects and not English. This meant that it was more palatable for other teachers who may not have embraced the writing project in its infancy and demonstrated how raising standards in literacy is everyone's responsibility.

Results from the pupil perception interviews and surveys also reinforced the power of the writing project over those twelve months, with the majority claiming that they believed their writing had improved since September 2006, as well as recognising how different pieces of writing were being incorporated into their other subject areas. It was also the responses from the pupil perception interviews that formalised what the whole-school literacy objectives would be for the following academic year:

1) Spelling tests each week on key vocabulary
2) To use dictionaries in all lessons
3) Discursive writing in *science and maths*
4) To be allowed more time in all lessons for extended pieces of writing
5) *Handwriting*

Finally, in terms of quantifying the writing project's success, the KS3 optional SATS that the pupils completed in June 2007 proved that both Years 7 and 8 had made significant progress in the number of Level 5 and Level 6 scores that they had achieved when compared to the tests undertaken the year before. It was truly amazing to see how this teamwork and cohesive approach to LAC and SPAG had raised standards in literacy at that point.

Addressing the 'short-term impact' of literacy across the curriculum projects

By 2008 I had moved on in my career and the whole-school writing project lost momentum and indeed seemed to fit the 'short-term impact' (Ofsted: 2013) outlined in the *Moving English on* report. Although I know that many departments had taken the findings from the writing project seriously and continued to embed them into their subjects, it needed someone to continue to oversee the development of the project. In retrospect, I should have delegated a series of roles to those non-English teachers who were keen to move this LAC project forwards so that the future success of the project did not singularly rely on one person overseeing the project.

Auditing English subject knowledge across the curriculum using 'English appendix 1: Spelling' and 'English appendix 2: vocabulary, grammar and punctuation', in the same way as auditing the department, might be the way in which a whole-school literacy project does not lose momentum. Since the writing project between 2006 and 2007, I have always believed that somebody who is not an English specialist teacher but is confident with their English subject knowledge would be best to lead such a programme. The one thing I learned from the writing project was that teachers were far more open to raising standards in literacy if the message was delivered by someone other than a member of the English department.

If I was ever fortunate enough to be part of such a project again, I would suggest that Figure 6.3 would be the ideal way of linking a LAC project with any proposed KS3 English model.

Delegating roles so that every department has a member who is solely responsible for overseeing LAC in their subject area and feeding it through to one non-specialist English teacher who then liaises with the KS3 English coordinator to see what the speaking and listening, reading and writing priorities are in the planning cycle means that no one person is driving the project forward. If someone in Figure 6.3 were to leave the school, then there would be a large enough pool of teachers to continue to move a LAC project forward until a replacement member of staff is found. This is all theory based on my own experiences. However, it is easy to become disillusioned when different types of LAC projects fizzle out simply because they lose momentum due to

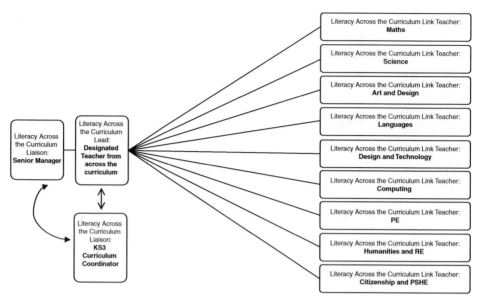

Figure 6.3 Literacy across the curriculum.

issues around staffing. If I were to repeat the experience of the writing project, I would make sure that I got all the staff in Figure 6.3 working together cohesively before launching any new LAC initiative on the school.

The whole-school writing project between 2006 and 2007 which focused on SPAG is only one element of LAC. Yet, SPAG is the easiest starting point in which departments can work together to help raise standards in English. With regards to LAC, in the *Key Stage 3: The wasted years?* report it says:

> In around 50% of the 200 monitoring inspections, inspectors identified that leaders were beginning to drive improvements at KS3. Evidence shows that the development of pupils' literacy skills was the most common area of improvement.
>
> (Ofsted: September 2015)

Although this is a positive step in the right direction, this quotation also suggests that at least 50% of the schools under the scrutiny of Ofsted during the monitoring visits were not driving improvements at KS3, including the 'development of pupils' literacy skills'. Therefore, if the straightforward nature of SPAG is used as a whole-school starting point by applying the audit, then at least efforts are being made to start raising standards in English in schools where, in the past, it hasn't proved to be the most important whole-school priority.

Issues surrounding the declining standards in English are not a new phenomenon for twenty-first century secondary schools. In 1975, *A Language for life* stated:

Many allegations about lower standards today come from employers, who maintain that young people joining them from school cannot write grammatically, are poor spellers, and generally express themselves badly. The employers sometimes draw upon past experience for comparisons, but even where they do there is a strong implication that at one time levels of performance was superior. It is therefore interesting to find in the Newbolt Report of 1921 observations of a very similar kind. There Messers Vickers Ltd reported 'great difficulty in obtaining junior clerks who can speak and write English clearly and correctly, especially those aged from 15 to 16 year's'.

(A Language for Life: 1975, p. 3)

These ironic parallels with the current situation where society perceives that young people are somehow deficient in their English skills cannot be ignored. In my experience, there is no one LAC project that fits all schools as one size does not fit all. Building cohesion and strengthening teamwork, however, across the curriculum is one way in which all teachers can strive to make society's perception that there is widespread illiteracy amongst pupils such as those school leavers from the 1920s, 1970s and 2010s referred to in this chapter become something of the past.

Notes

1 *A language for life:* Report of the committee of enquiry appointed by the Secretary of State for Education and Science under the chairmanship of Sir Alan Bullock FBA, Department of Education and Science, 1975, p. 4.
2 *Moving English forward: Action to raise standards in English*, Ofsted, April 2013; https://www.gov.uk/government/publications/moving-english-forward.
3 *Statutory guidance: National curriculum in England: English programmes of study*, Department for Education, September 2013 (updated, July 2014); https://www.gov.uk/government/publications/national-curriculum-in-england-english-programmes-of-study.
4 *Assessing Pupil Progress (APP) in English*, Department for Children, Schools and Families, August 2008; http://webarchive.nationalarchives.gov.uk/20110113104120; http://nationalstrategies.standards.dcsf.gov.uk/node/16051?uc=force_uj.

CHAPTER 7

Speaking and listening in the Key Stage 3 English curriculum

In a book that is dedicated to raising the profile of KS3 English and putting it at the heart of a department's agenda, it seems irregular to begin a chapter discussing KS4. However, to understand the significance of the role played by speaking and listening in the current KS3 English programmes of study, it is important to begin by reflecting upon the impact that the removal of the 20% speaking and listening segment from GCSE English and English language has had on its deemed worth at KS3.

The politicising of speaking and listening in English at KS4 and its impact on KS3 English

Following consecutive scandalous revelations in the English media that GCSEs in English and English language were somehow fixed, open to cheating and even worse, much easier than the O-Level English exams that were sat by pupils two to three generations ago, the Office of Qualifications and Exam Regulations (Ofqual) responded to increasing political and media pressure by producing a 'Consultation on the Removal of Speaking and Listening Assessment from GCSE English and GCSE English Language' in April 2013. Central to this consultation was the following announcement:

> We are proposing that performance in speaking and listening will no longer contribute to the overall mark and grade achieved by a student. Instead, results will be calculated from the other component parts of the qualification.
>
> If these proposals are implemented, then from 2014 students would achieve GCSE grades calculated without reference to their speaking and listening performance.[1]

The other 'component parts of the qualification' Ofqual refers to are reading and writing. Consequently, English teachers across England, already under immeasurable pressure to perform well in national league tables and under the scrutiny of a difficult Ofsted agenda, may possibly veer towards teaching how to successfully answer reading and writing questions in the exam in order to help their pupils achieve the best possible GCSE grades at the end of KS4. It could also be suggested that the proposal responded to wider political pressures when, in the consultation, Ofqual stated:

> *there are no practical arrangements that we consider we can make to ensure assessment of speaking and listening is sufficiently resilient. Therefore, we are proposing a different approach – to remove speaking and listening from the pressures of the accountability measures.*

(Ofqual: April 2013)

This statement 'to remove speaking and listening' not only overtly appeared to reduce its importance, but also had the effect, inadvertently and subconsciously, of relegating its importance in the classroom because English teachers would need to dedicate their time to getting the pupils successfully through the reading and writing tasks that were set either in an exam or under controlled assessment conditions.

Coincidently, as well as the proposed date for the removal of speaking and listening from the English and English Language GCSE, in September of 2014, the new statutory KS3 English Programmes of Study were also implemented. As I gazed through the draft proposals and the final revisions before September 2014, it became quite clear that speaking and listening had already been relegated in its academic standing. Even though 'Spoken Language' and its importance is acknowledged in the opening to the 2014 English KS3 programme of study, in terms of the 'Subject Content'[2] to be delivered by teachers, it now ranks below reading, writing, grammar and vocabulary and rests at the end of the final page.

The history of speaking and listening in the KS3 English National Curriculum in England

Since my fledgling days as a trainee teacher, speaking and listening was the very first thing to appear on the content to be delivered section in the statutory English Programmes of Study from KS1 to KS4. In 1999, the 'Key stage 3 programme of study: English'[3] physically placed speaking and listening above reading and writing in the content to be delivered and was referred to as 'EN1', whilst also stating that 'Teaching should ensure that work in speaking and listening, *reading* and *writing* is integrated' (DFES: 2004), suggesting that there was an equality shared across the three disciplines. When the proceeding National Curriculum was launched in 2010, speaking and listening also physically headed the list above reading and writing in the teaching of the key processes,[4] range and content and curriculum opportunities that formed the content for the 'Programme of study for Key Stage 3 and attainment targets' in English.

Symbolically, the fact that speaking and listening was physically at the head of these statutory content descriptors within the KS3 English programmes of study – with significant attention to detail separately given to both 'Speaking' and 'Listening' in the skill descriptors – suggested that without high-quality speaking and listening tasks a pupil could be at a disadvantage in terms of how well they understood the texts that they would study; additionally, it also suggested that pupils needed clear opportunities to verbalise their ideas before actually writing them down. In retrospect, I believe that the title should have been 'Listening and speaking', as listening precedes speaking – it is the first thing that happens to a person in utero and is possibly the single most important social and academic skill that a human develops during their lifetime.

Even more startling than this lower ranking status in the 2014 programmes of study content descriptors was the decision to use the term 'Spoken English', which has now replaced 'Speaking and listening' as a named heading in the new English national curriculum. It is significant because the removal of 'listening' suggests that this crucial social and academic skill is not deemed important enough to be referred to in the 2014 KS3 English Programmes of Study. Having taught both GCSE English language and A-Level English language, I immediately associated the term 'Spoken English' with audio transcriptions, syntax trees and sociolinguistics and not with the art of discussion, reflection and debate. As such, it would be easier to concede and 'teach to the test' by designing a KS3 curriculum model that helped pupils practise the reading and writing exam skills that they would need by the end of KS4.

However, with this proposed curriculum model that I am advocating, speaking and listening is not mentioned as a peripheral topic, nor is it referred to as 'Spoken language'. Rather, it forms an integral part of KS3 English planning at every level and remains very much at the heart of the proposed KS3 English curriculum model. It has equal weighting and is part of a curriculum that is 'distinctive, innovative and planned very well to meet pupils' needs in reading, writing, speaking and listening'.[5]

Speaking and Listening and the importance of planning high-quality tasks

In June 2007, I attended an inspirational seminar on 'Who talks? The big issues' led by Professor Debra Myhill (Pro-Vice-Chancellor and Executive Dean: University of Exeter). By the end of the seminar, Professor Myhill helped me to realise just how important it was to plan high-quality speaking and listening tasks in my own lessons. Furthermore, the seminar prompted me to become conscious of how much talking I did during a lesson at the expense of the pupils who often have a lot of interesting and more important things to say to each other as well as to me. In response to this self-realisation, I wanted to become more confident in building opportunities for high-quality speaking and listening tasks into my daily planning (where it was appropriate) so that the pupils were able to develop their speaking and listening skills in order that they could become autonomous learners. Seven years later and in the early stages of the planning cycle (Chapter 2), the positioning of high-quality speaking and listening tasks now had to be transferred from my individual lesson plans into the proposed curriculum model.

Speaking and listening and long-term planning

In terms of the long-term plan outlined in Table 7.1, there is clear reference to Speaking and Listening as a priority as it is one of the formal assessment tasks for autumn 2 and is clearly marked in the Year 7 column. By the end of autumn 2, pupils are asked to take part in a group performance of a ballad that they have studied. At this point it may, in terms of national priorities, seem more appropriate to instruct the Year 7 pupils to complete a written essay that closely focuses on the structure, imagery and themes of a ballad. However, if the speaking and listening task is structured well, with overarching guidance from the KS3 English coordinator, and is carefully planned and prepared by the individual teacher based on the needs of their class, there is no reason why a formal speaking and listening task cannot supersede a written task in terms of accurately monitoring an individual pupil's understanding of the ballad's structure, imagery and themes. As well as the example of the Year 7 speaking and listening task in autumn 2, there are also formal speaking and listening assessments for Year 8 in Spring 2 and Year 9 in summer 2; these too are clearly marked on the respective long-term plans.

If a KS3 English teacher wants their pupils to formally record the speaking and listening assessment, then they – or their department – could adopt a pro forma similar to the one exemplified in Table 7.2.

This is a generic pro forma that can be used across KS3 English at any time. Often, a summative score, grade, term or level is also needed, but that is dependent on the individual department's assessment policy. Taking the example of the Year 7 speaking and listening assessment from Table 7.1, it is clear that the pro forma is not designed as a formal way of assessing whether the pupil understands the aforementioned ballad's structure, imagery and themes.

81

Table 7.1 Speaking and listening long-term plan

Key Stage 3 English: 2016-2017: Autumn 2

Year 7	Year 8	Year 9
Words, Sounds, Images Revision of Poetry Across Time: Medieval to the Victorians (4 Weeks + 3Weeks A1)	*Words, Sounds, Images* Revision and progression upon the different approaches to seen and unseen poetry (3 Weeks+3Weeks A1)	*Words, Sounds, Images* Secure knowledge of the different approaches to seen and unseen poetry (4 weeks+3Weeks A1)
Unit Name: *Shaking Up the Senses!* (**Text Types:** Multi-Modal, Still Images, Pop Music Lyrics, Different Types of Poems)	**Unit Name:** *Questioning the Voice in Contemporary Poetry* (**Text Types:** Post-Modern Poetry, Multi-Modal, Still Images, Recount, Commentary, Autobiography)	**Unit Name:** *Why War?* (**Text Types:** Multi-Modal, Still Images, Report, Recount, Biography, Propaganda, Speech, WW1 Poetry, Timelines, Letters, Commentary)
	Library Lesson: Year 7 Group Readers: **Guided Reading Activities (Differentiated)**	
Cauldron of Characterisation Revision of the differences between direct and indirect characterisation with close attention to the language of Dickens (3 Weeks)	*Cauldron of Characterisation* Analysis of a range of different characters across a range of short stories by Roald Dahl (4 Weeks)	*Cauldron of Characterisation* Secure knowledge and perceptive analysis of Conan-Doyle's Famous Detective (pre and post 20th-century character evaluations of the representation of Sherlock Holmes) (3Weeks)
Unit Name: *Will the real Scrooge Please stand up?* (**Text Types:** Multi-Modal, Still Images, Differentiated Prose, Script, Biography)	**Unit Name:** *Being a Detective!* (**Text Types:** Short Stories, Multi-Modal, Still Images, Biography, Newspaper Reports)	**Unit Name:** *It's All Elementary!* (**Text Types:** Multi-Modal, Still Images, Differentiated Prose, Biography, Newspaper Reports)
	Library Lesson: Year 8 Class Reader: **Guided Reading Activities (Differentiated)**	
		Library Lesson: Year 9 Class Reader **Guided Reading Activities (Differentiated)**
SPAG Lesson: Weekly (A2) Sp: To Consolidate and Secure our knowledge of Year 3 – 6 Spelling Lists (*Challenge:* Spelling Challenge and Preparatory Spelling Bee List) **P:** To revise different methods to avoid comma splicing **G:** To secure our understanding of: Relative clauses; Modal Verbs and Adverbs; Adverbials (**SEN:** Secure understanding of subject-verb-object)	**SPAG Lesson: Fortnightly (A2): Sp:** Securing knowledge of complex polysyllabic words by focusing on prefixes and suffixes (*Challenge:* Spelling Challenge and Preparatory Spelling Bee List) **P:** Ensuring Accuracy and Variety **G:** Revising the appropriateness of syntax in formal and informal texts.	**SPAG Lesson: Fortnightly (A2): Sp:** Consolidation and secure knowledge of complex syllabic and irregular spelt words **P:** Consolidation and Secure knowledge of punctuation as well as using sophisticated punctuation techniques for effect in writing. **G:** Ensuring secure use of sentence variety to create certain effects in writing.
Assessment Tasks for Autumn 2: Speaking and Listening: *Group Performance of a Ballad*	**Assessment Tasks for Autumn 2:** Writing: *Write the opening paragraphs for a detective story* (See Sequence of Learning for differentiated task)	**Assessment Tasks for Autumn 2** Reading: *Comparing and Contrasting values in the poetry of the First World War* (See Sequence of Learning for differentiated tasks)
GCSE Assessment Objectives Covered: Language: Writing: Paper 1: Imaginary Writing (AO5) **Reading:** Close Analysis of Language and Structure (AO2)	**GCSE Assessment Objectives Covered: Language: Writing:** Paper 1: Imaginary Writing (AO5/AO6) **Reading:** Close Analysis of Language and Structure (AO2) **Literature:** Poetry Comparison (AO1 and AO2)	**GCSE Assessment Objectives Covered: Language: Writing:** Paper 2: Writing to Inform/Explain (AO5 and AO6) **Reading:** Close Analysis of Language/Structure (AO2) **Literature:** Contextual Poetry Comparison (AO2 and AO3)
PLTS: Let's Think in English Lesson: *Jabberwocky* Reasoning Pattern: Classification (**Withdrawn from the LTE Programme. As such, will change in 2017 review**)	**PLTS:** Let's Think in English Lesson: *The Open Window.* Reasoning pattern: Narrative Sequencing	**PLTS:** Let's Think in English Lesson: *The Last Days of Okawa* Reasoning pattern: Narrative Sequencing

Christmas Holidays

Table 7.2 Assessment feedback sheet

KS3 English: Formative Assessment Feedback Sheet: Speaking and Listening					
Unit of Work:					
What was the task?					
Circle the areas (below) that were being assessed					
Talking to others	Listening to others	Talking with others	Responding to others	Talking within drama and role play	Talking about Talk

Who assessed you? (Underline)	Peer / Teacher / Both

What did they say your strengths were? (Up to 3)	
1.	
2.	
3.	
Do you agree with these strengths? (**Challenge: Can you explain** why?)	

What **one** target were you given to help you improve your speaking and listening skills?

Rather, it is a way for the pupil to practise difficult skills such as evaluating and justifying which are equally, if not more, important for the pupil when they finally enter the world of work. With the more challenging classes that I have taught across KS3 English, I have found it useful to actually teach them what a good listener looks and sounds like quite early on in the autumn term. It may seem quite a basic thing to do at the beginning of the year; however, in my experience, I have found that a gentle or robust reminder of these crucial skills (depending on the class) really does help the pupils when it comes to the process of self-reflection of their listening skills, whether they are completing a pro forma or not.

Speaking and listening and medium-term planning

As outlined in Chapter 2, there are certain elements from the long-term plan that are reproduced in the medium-term plan. Speaking and listening and, in particular, the Personal Learning and Thinking Skills (PLTS) that occur on the autumn 2 long-term plan (see Table 7.1) also have a prominent section on the medium-term plan, where it states that the *'Let's think in English'* lesson is a mandatory lesson that must take place at the beginning of the sequence of learning (see Table 7.3).

A number of English teachers from the department went on the training for the *Let's think in English*[6] programme in 2012, led by Laurie Smith and Michael Walsh from King's College, London. By 2014 and in the early stages of the planning cycle, it was clearly accepted across the department that it was imperative that these self-contained, fortnightly lessons had to be a mandatory part of any curriculum model that would be produced. This is because the range and difficulty of the texts in the *Let's think in English* lessons and the high quality of the ensuing pupil discussion across a range of abilities at KS3 supports the pupils in becoming autonomous learners. From firsthand experience, the 'structured group discussion' and 'structured challenge' (Smith and Walsh: August 2016) allows the pupils to verbalise their ideas in meaningful discussion with each other.

This combination of independent learning and peer support that is fused within the *Let's think in English* lessons crosses a range of demographics and helps the 'verbal drafting' process (see Figure 7.1) that Smith and Walsh refer to. I have also seen firsthand how these lessons directly help the pupils in their writing practice. For example, reluctant writers often can't wait to put pen to paper once they have the confidence in their own ideas as they have already been verbalised and often validated by their peers – in my experience, their self-belief rockets following a *Let's think in English* lesson.

Table 7.3 Let's think in English lesson plan.

Autumn 1/2 Medium-Term Plan: **Year 9: *Words, Sounds, Images***	
Unit Name: Why War?	**Duration:** 7 Weeks: **A1** (3 Weeks) **A2** (4 Weeks)
Learning Cycle	**Overview of unit (National Curriculum Subject Content):**
5. Assessing 1: Knowledge 2. Skills — 1. KWHL — 2. Different Text Types — 3. Independent Learning — 4. Feedback	Pupils will be expected to **(NC)** *Speak confidently and effectively through giving short speeches and presentations, expressing their own ideas and keeping to point.* Furthermore, they will have the opportunity to **(NC)** *participate in formal debates and structured discussions* whilst also being able to **(NC)** *improvise, rehearse and play scripts and poetry in order to discuss language use and meaning.* Pupils will secure their critical skills when recognising how **(NC)** *figurative language, vocabulary choice, grammar, text structure and organisational features, present meaning.* Furthermore, pupils will be expected to **(NC)** *write accurately, fluently and at length for pleasure and information* by **(NC)** *amending the vocabulary, grammar and structure of their writing to improve its coherence and overall effectiveness.*
1. **KWHL** (What do I **k**now? What do I **w**ant to know? **H**ow will I learn?)	*How confident am I with the close analysis of a variety of text types? *How well can I compare two texts whilst also forging a critical argument? *How will my existing knowledge of War, particularly World War One, help in my understanding of a writer's viewpoint and attitude? *How will I develop my empathy skills and understanding of war literature?
2. **Different Text Types**	Students begin to respond to the different elements within stage one of the learning cycle by responding to a range of different text types including: Multi-Modal, Still Images, Report, Recount, Biography, Propaganda, Speech, WW1 Poetry, Timelines, Letters, Commentary
3. **Independent Learning**	To work through the skills in the success criteria using a range of independent learning strategies including: active reading; summative tests such as: quizzes, word searches etc; formative self and peer-assessment of written work.
4. **Feedback**	Speaking and Listening: For example, Socratic discussion of issues within the literature studied; hot-seating of characters; tableaus.
5. **Assessing Knowledge and Skills**	Comparative Essay; Close analysis of a non-fiction text (See *Sequence of Learning* for details of tasks)
6. KWHL (What have I learned during this unit?)	Response to stage one of the learning cycle; response to success criteria; create a summary/poster/poem about *what I have learned during this unit.*
Success Criteria	

- To **explore** how writers of the war genre use a range of techniques, including writing and sentence choices, to affect the reader (**Low Level Skill**)
- To **experiment** with language and sentence styles appropriate to the war genre in creative writing and analytical writing (**Mid-Level Skill**)
- To **evaluate** and **critically choose** from a range of imaginative, flexible sentence structures to use for deliberate effect in both creative and analytical writing (**High-Level Skill**)

Table 7.3 (Continued).

Differentiation	
Support	*All paper resources to be on cream/light blue paper with a minimum of 12+ Comic Sans/ Arial font-type and all projected resources to be on a cream/light blue background with Comic Sans/Arial font-type set at a minimum of 28+ with fewer words and symbols/images to support key words, terms and ideas for those pupils who experience a barrier to reading written texts. *Guided and independent reading using fiction and non-fiction cue cards: Focus on word level, working up to sentence level questions and tasks in guided reading groups. Even within the lower sets, the pupils will be grouped according to ability with colour-coded tasks to support differentiation *The provision of writing frames in extended writing tasks *Adopting roles in speaking and listening tasks that students feel confident with. *Socratic dialogue to boost confidence in formal group discussion as the pupils are there to support each other. Although the teacher may choose a straightforward class debate arrangement to encourage discussion as this is a more familiar discursive set-up. *Active reading strategies to help the pupils engage with unseen texts. *There is an alternative scheme of work available in this unit that is specifically designed to help pupils consolidate what they have learned at a steady pace. However, pupils will also be able to access a whole range of differentiated resources within the main sequence of learning as well. *The reading assessment is clearly structured with prompts and focuses on the close analysis **of one poem**.
Challenge	* Guided and independent reading using fiction and non-fiction cue cards: pupils to focus on sentence and text level questions and tasks. **Choice and Challenge:** Pupils to independently choose from a number of colour-coded guided questions and activities from across the range of guided and independent reading fiction and non-fiction cue cards. *Pupils will have the option to choose from a range of challenge activities in lessons and for homework. *Pupils will be grouped for guided reading and writing tasks according to their confidence and ability; however, there will be a great deal of focus on independent learning during sustained pieces of writing. *The reading assessment has few prompts and asks to compare two poems in detail. *All pupils are encouraged to vary their roles in Socratic discussion to develop their speaking and listening skills.

SPAG	**Sp**: Consolidation and secure knowledge of complex syllabic and irregular spelt words **P**: Consolidation and Secure knowledge of punctuation as well as using sophisticated punctuation techniques for effect in writing. **G:** Ensuring secure use of sentence variety to create certain effects in writing.
PLTS (Mandatory: To take place at the beginning of the sequence of learning)	Let's Think in English Lesson: The Last Days of Okawa. Reasoning pattern: Narrative Sequencing; Socratic Discussion
Links to other areas of the Curriculum:	History/Geography/PSHE/Religious Studies/Science/Art
Homework	See *Sequence of Learning*
SMSC: This Scheme of Work prepares our young people to move into the world of work and function fully as citizens to their community in which they live by:	Exploring experiences and respecting the values of others whilst also discovering themselves and the surrounding world and their place within it. They will be asked to respond to the array of texts with creativity and reflection including being able to recognise right from wrong and understanding the consequences of the choices that they may make. This scheme of work also promotes the British values of democracy, individual liberty and mutual respect and tolerance The unit coincides with the Royal British Legion's *Festival of Remembrance* marking the armistice of the First World War on November 11th.
Gender	It is easy to assume that the 'war' genre is stereotypically preferred by boys. However, this scheme of work begins by looking at the effects of war on <u>all</u> children who experience such horrors both a hundred years ago and presently in places such as the Middle East. <u>All</u> pupils will be required to develop their empathy skills and understand the suffering and hope that takes place by children who find themselves in a war-torn situation. They will also learn about the loss of a generation in Britain that took place exactly 100 years ago by looking at two First World War poetry anthologies from the perspective of both male and female writers.

The Let's Think in English programme has been developed since 2009, closely modelled on Adey and Shayer's Cognitive Acceleration in Science Education (CASE).

Cognitive Acceleration (CA) is one of only two interventions whose effectiveness in significantly raising attainment has been repeatedly proven in international trials over 20+ years: the other two is Feuerstein's Instrumental Enrichment. CA is based on concepts from Piaget and Vygotsky, chiefly the social construction of understanding through structured group discussion and raising of students' "zone of proximal development" through structured challenge

CA, especially CASE, became increasing widely established in England during the 1980s and 1990s, but was squeezed out of school curriculums by the National Strategies from 1997 and by an increasingly heavy demand for frequent assessment and tracking of progress. By 2008 it had been become apparent from international surveys of student attainment (PISA, PIRLS and TIMSS) that attainment in English schools was not rising.

From 2008 there was a commitment, shared by all the main political parties, to raising standards of attainment in English schools towards those of more successful countries and to reducing the 'tail' of students leaving school with poor qualifications or none. These overarching aims were set out in the foreword to the Coalition Government's White Paper, *The Importance of Teaching* (November 2010) and remain current Government and cross-party policies. It was apparent that they would require, among other reforms, more effective teaching of moderately and less able students and more demanding GCSE examinations. For English this would require students to respond more effectively to more challenging seen and unseen texts and more open-ended questions needing higher cognitive skills and greater confidence.

King's College London, where CA had originated, therefore decided to develop a CA programme for English to mirror those in Science and Maths for which a revival was expected. This began in 2009 and was led by Laurie Smith and Michael Walsh, supervised by Philip Adey, with development focussed on Years 7 and 8. Following successful trialling of the CA Key Stage 3 English lessons, further lessons have been developed specifically for GCSE and for Key Stages 1 and 2.

The KS3 programme consists of 30+ lessons all using English texts – fiction, poetry, non-fiction and film – with others designed for GCSE and Key Stages 1 and 2. The lessons stimulate the deeper reasoning patterns which underpin understanding of English texts – classification, frame of reference, writer's intentions and methods, genre, symbolism and narrative structure. They systematically develop students' skills of inference, deduction and analysis, increasing their confidence, resilience, understanding and ability to express their ideas effectively. The focus on structured group discussion and feedback has been described as 'verbal drafting'.

Laurie Smith and Michael Walsh (King's College, London: August 2016)

Figure 7.1

At this point, it is extremely important to highlight that the *Let's think in English* lessons are instructed to take place fortnightly in order for them to have maximum impact in terms of successive outcomes. Currently in this proposed curriculum model, as shown in Table 7.2 and 7.3, the pupils are expected to complete a mandatory *Let's think in English* lesson half-termly every six to seven weeks. This is not an ideal situation in terms of the proven pedagogy that lies behind the *Let's think in English* programme outlined by Smith and Walsh in Figure 7.1. Although 18 mandatory *Let's think in English* lessons currently form part of the proposed KS3 English curriculum model at the moment,

English teachers are actively encouraged to draw from the full bank of 30-plus lessons that are regularly updated by Laurie Smith and Michael Walsh. It is hoped that staff feedback with regard to their use of *Let's think in English* lessons throughout the year will enable the department to decide collaboratively where other opportunities to further embed this proved cognitive approach to learning might lie.

Speaking and listening and the sequence of learning

As well as the mandatory *Let's think in English* lessons clearly being labelled in the long- and medium-term plans for autumn 1/2, they are also highlighted at the beginning of each sequence of learning, as demonstrated in Table 7.4.

In addition to these mandatory *Let's think in English* lessons, there are also lots of other examples of high-quality speaking and listening tasks that feature in the sequence of learning in the 'Suggested Resources to help fulfil the Week's Learning Objectives' column. It is important to reiterate once again the focus on the term 'Suggested', because it is the responsibility of the teacher to plan what works for the class that they are teaching in the short term and not all of the tasks that are suggested in the sequence of learning will be appropriate for all of the pupils. Nevertheless, highlighting when and where there may be opportunities for more formal speaking and listening tasks to take place within the sequence of learning (whether they be discussion based, role-play or individual speaking) encourages the department to think about using high-quality speaking and listening tasks in their own teaching.

One example of a high-quality speaking and listening task that features in a number of sequences of learning across this proposed KS3 English curriculum model is Socratic discussion, which is based on the ancient principles laid down by Socrates where the teacher is the 'leader' and offers an open-ended question before facilitating the ensuing pupil debate. These are not arbitrary open-ended questions; rather, they are intrinsic to the overall scheme of work and aid the students in their understanding of the texts that they are studying as it helps them verbalise their ideas and respond constructively to the opinions of others in a supportive environment.

I first used the Socratic inner/outer circle (or Socratic seminar) approach to whole-class discussion in my own lessons in 2007 following my attendance on the course 'Who talks? The big issues'. Professor Myhill had provided examples and demonstrated how Socratic discussion can work successfully in the classroom and can be pitched to pupils across a range of abilities. Even though it took a number of attempts to build the pupils' confidence as well as my own

Table 7.4 Sequence of learning: Year 9 words, sounds images: Why war?

Week	Learning Objectives	Suggested Resources to help fulfil the Week's Learning Objectives	Suggested Homework
1	PLTS: Let's Think Lesson: *The Last Days of Okawa* Reasoning pattern: Narrative Sequencing (Mandatory Lesson and PPT on VLE)		
	1. To **recall** any knowledge that the pupil may have on war photography or war literature (**Low-Level Skill**) 2. To **compare** and **contrast** different war photographs (**Mid-Level Skill**) 3. To **construct** and self or peer **appraise** a piece of descriptive writing based on a war photograph using a sensory language criterion (**High-Level Skills**)	• **KWH**L (What do I **k**now? What do I **w**ant to know? **H**ow will I learn?) These grids can take any form that the teacher thinks will work best for their class (e.g. In their exercise books; on A3 paper hanging from learning lines using post-it notes; using ICT). This can be individual/paired/group work with feedback. Make sure that the last column is clear ready to be completed at the end of the unit (NB. This column can also be completed alongside the student's learning journey too as part of a plenary activity). • **Famous War Photographs:** See the *Staff Shared Network* area for suggested pictures. There is a sample from famous paintings through to WW1 photography through to contemporary war pictures of war in more recent history) Students to question the pictures (**Differentiation: Support:** Provide examples of questions that the students may ask. **Challenge:** Students to focus on the higher-level questioning such as *how?* and *why?* In groups students to answer each other's questions. • **Descriptive Writing:** Students to choose one of the photographs and zoom in, using sensory language to describe what they see (**Differentiation: Support:** Writing Frames with one assigned picture. **Challenge:** Students to use two pictures and work on sophisticated juxtaposition of images) • **Homework feedback**: Hot seating activity: War Photographer	Prepare at least five questions **Differentiation: Support:** Provide a couple of examples and then ask the students to write at least three questions. **Challenge:** (With suggested answers) that you would like to ask a war photographer **Challenge:** Research a famous war photographer(s) and write a 200 word (300 words for comparative) summary **Challenge: And/or** Choose another picture that you have studied within the unit so far and either: write a further piece of descriptive writing and/or write a newspaper report to accompany the image.

when trialling Socratic discussion, it is now something that I use regularly across Key Stages 3 and 4.

Once more, in the early stages of the planning cycle, I proposed that Socratic discussion should feature in as many of the KS3 English schemes of work as possible because it had proved to be successful in my own and others' teaching.

Although there are recommended open-ended questions in the 'Suggested Resources to help fulfil the Week's Learning Objectives' (see Tables 7.5 and 7.6) across the various sequences of learning in Years 7, 8 and 9, the classroom teacher might choose to adapt, add to or even change the question according to the needs of their particular class.

One particular member of the department, Sarah Lovell-Brown, developed Socratic discussion so positively in their KS3 English classes that when I approached them about the possibility of making a training video for the department, they were eager to show our colleagues just how successful a learning tool it can be. This collaboration means that the training video and guidelines are available for all teachers to see so that they can begin trialling Socratic discussion with their own classes. For new teachers, the departmental training video on Socratic discussion and any guidance for the suggested speaking and listening activities are clearly highlighted on the sequence of learning, as exemplified in the Year 7 lesson on Table 7.5 and Year 8 lesson on Table 7.6.

Table 7.5 Spring 1: Sequence of learning: Year 7: A novel idea! Looking at innocence and experience in the Year 7 set text.

Week	Learning Objectives	Suggested Resources to help fulfil the Week's Learning Objectives	Suggested Homework
4	1. To **identify** the main arguments in the home-school debate **(Low Level Skill)** 2. To **develop** these ideas about the home-school debate and **organise** them into arguments and counter-arguments **(Mid-Level Skills)** 3. To **appraise** the ideas of others and **justify** our responses about the home-school debate during a Socratic discussion **(High Level Skills)**	• To read chapters 11–23 of the novel (Audiobook option on the *Staff Shared Network* area) • Shared reading followed by guided reading activities **(Support:** Yellow for characterisation with increasing challenge across abilities to **Challenge**: grey for structure and blue for hooks) • **Speaking and Listening:** *Socratic Discussion:* Question: *Why do parents choose to educate their children at home?* **(Support:** Debate: *Which do you think is the best idea: learning at home or learning at school? Can you give at least three reasons why?)* Resources for the speaking and listening tasks can be found on the *Staff Shared Network* area. *Further guidance on organising a Socratic discussion can be found on the *Staff Shared Network* area where you can also watch the departmental training video: *How to organise a Socratic discussion*	**Scheme of Work Homework Project (Week 4):** William Blake **(Challenge!** and the Romantics) Writing to Inform; Explain; Describe (See homework project sheet for exact details.) **Further Challenge** To create a list of 10 questions that you would like to ask the novella's female protagonist. Next, choose the best 5 questions from your list and justify your reasons for choosing them.

Table 7.6 Summer 1: Sequence of learning: Year 8: All the world's a stage! Examining prejudice in Shakespeare's 'The Merchant of Venice'.

Week	Learning Objectives	Suggested Resources to help fulfil the Week's Learning Objectives	Suggested Homework
5	1. To **identify** the generic characteristics of a villain (antagonist) **(Low-Level Skill)** 2. To **choose** examples from the play where Shylock may be depicted as a victim or as a villain by Shakespeare **(Mid-Level Skill)** 3. To **justify** decisions made about the nature of Shylock's character **(High-Level Skill)**	• Drama activities on Shylock's monologue: *I am a Jew*. A range of differentiated dramatic activities can be found on the VLE for further exploration. • **Speaking and Listening:** *Socratic Discussion:* Question: *Do you feel sorry for Shylock? Discuss* (**Support:** (For example, organising your classroom like a courtroom so there is the prosecution and defence) *Do you think that Shylock is a victim or a villain? Can you give at least three reasons why?*) Resources for the speaking and listening tasks can be found on the VLE. *Further guidance on organising a Socratic discussion can be found on the VLE where you can also watch the departmental training video: How to organise a Socratic discussion* • Pupils to organise their ideas ready for the reading assessment that will take place over the next week. Offer different examples of learning tools (e.g. mind maps; double-bubble graphs) so that pupils are able to begin to structure their essay. Peer assessment of ideas. **Support:** Provide writing frames to help pupils organise their ideas plus a bank of coordinating and subordinating conjunctions to help pupils link their ideas.	**Support** In preparation for their debate/role play, pupils are to prepare between 2 to 5 questions with possible answers that they can use in the whole-class discussion about whether Shylock is a villain or victim. (They can then transfer these ideas into their reading assessments if they wish) **Challenge** Pupils to begin drafting an introduction to their reading assessment ready for peer assessment (**Support:** Depending on the class it might be worth giving pupils some generic guidance about how to respond to essay questions)

Examples of differentiated speaking and listening tasks in the proposed KS3 English curriculum model

Tables 7.5 and 7.6 also show how there is a differentiated speaking and listening task suggested as an alternative to the Socratic discussion for those classes that need more structure and support when contributing to whole-class discussion. Even though the Socratic seminar involves all students in the class, the fact that it is facilitated rather than directed by the teacher means that it may not suit pupils who need specific guidance and extra support in class. Providing a structured alternative to the Socratic discussion, alongside dramatic tasks, as well as the *Let's think in English* lessons, means that all pupils are provided with opportunities to participate in a range of individual or collaborative undertakings that helps them to value the importance of speaking and listening in their own learning.

Notes

1 *Consultation on the Removal of Speaking and Listening Assessment from GCSE English and GCSE English Language*, Ofqual, April 2013; http://webarchive.nationalarchives.gov.uk/+/http://comment.ofqual.gov.uk/speaking-and-listening/.

2 *Statutory guidance: National curriculum in England: English programmes of study, Department for Education*, September 2013 (updated, July 2014); https://www.gov.uk/government/publications/national-curriculum-in-england-english-programmes-of-study.

3 *The National Curriculum: Handbook for Secondary Teachers in England*, Department for Education and Skills, 1999 (revised, October 2004); http://webarchive.nationalarchives.gov.uk/20130401151715/http://www.education.gov.uk/publications/eOrderingDownload/QCA-04-1374.pdf.

4 *English: Programme of study for key stage 3 and attainment targets (This is an extract from The National Curriculum 2007)*, Qualifications and Curriculum Authority, 2007; http://webarchive.nationalarchives.gov.uk/20100823130703/http://curriculum.qcda.gov.uk/uploads/QCA-07-3332-pEnglish3_tcm8-399.pdf.

5 *Moving English forward: Action to raise standards in English*, Ofsted, April 2013; https://www.gov.uk/government/publications/moving-english-forward.

6 Smith, Laurie and Walsh, Michael, n.d. *Let's think in English*, London: King's College, London; https://www.letsthinkinenglish.org.

CHAPTER 8

Using multimodal texts in Key Stage 3 English

Like the term 'Speaking and listening', the words 'multimodal texts' and specific references to the 'media' are also inauspiciously missing from the current KS3 English programmes of study. Furthermore, these notable absences are reflected in KS4 English. Specific analysis and the examination of a pupil's understanding of a media text, is no longer a component of the new GCSE English Language specification. It feels like multimodal texts, as well as speaking and listening, are no longer regarded as being integral to a pupil's understanding of English.

The KS3 English programme of study solely focuses on the pupil's ability to read and respond to actual written texts on a page, 'including in particular whole books, short stories, poems and plays with a wide coverage of genres, historical periods, forms and authors'.[1] The high level of content outlined in the programmes of study means that in terms of time, it would be difficult to incorporate the study of specific multimodal texts across Years 7, 8 and 9. However, in the KS3 English curriculum model that I am proposing, I will demonstrate how multimodal texts are not singularly used to enhance meaning in the works of literature outlined in the programmes of study; I will also discuss how vital it is to study specific multimodal texts in their entirety even though it is not a statutory requirement.

Why is it important to keep specific multimodal schemes of work in a KS3 English curriculum?

Having taught GCSE media studies for three years, in addition to teaching the media component of the old GCSE English specifications, I am the first to dismiss the myth that the teaching of multimodal texts such as films and TV adverts is easy when compared to the perceived rigour of the books, poems and plays that are listed in the literary canon. There is some notion that pupils simply have to watch multimodal texts in lessons and respond by completing tasks such as drawing a storyboard or writing a film review. Arbitrary follow-up tasks such as these do indeed lack challenge, but placed in the context of a multimodal scheme of work, they are not only meaningful but provide lots of rigorous learning.

Even though English teachers are under pressure to cover all of the different written text types outlined in the KS3 English programmes of study, the ability to access multimodal texts, resources and accompanying schemes of work is far easier than it was two years ago when the most recent National Curriculum was implemented. This is because English teachers understand the profound impact that teaching schemes of work specifically about multimodal texts has on their pupils, especially reluctant readers and writers and those who are disaffected with secondary school.

In the essay 'Digital Natives, Digital Immigrants' written in 2001, ten years after the first ever website went live in Europe, Marc Prensky discusses the differences between young people born into the technology age and those adults who weren't. Prensky summarises:

> *Our students today are all "native speakers" of the digital language of computers, video games and the Internet ... Those of us who were not born into the digital world ... are, and always will be compared to them, Digital Immigrants.*[2]

Prensky's assertion that the digital age is an intrinsic part of a young person is extremely important and relevant, especially when considering the current KS3 English programmes of study. Multimodal texts are a medium that is inclusive, as all pupils inherently understand and can respond with insight to the digital world that surrounds them. The fact that they are missing from the KS3 English programmes of study sends a silent message to the pupils that at best, the adults who decide what texts they will study are digital Luddites; at worst, there is an underlying arrogance that the only way young people can relate and empathise with society is through the medium of the written word. I am not suggesting that multimodal texts should suddenly replace the vast amount of literature outlined in the programmes of study. However, I believe that by omitting the term multimodal texts entirely it means that the KS3 English curriculum is not as rich and inclusive as it should be at the beginning of the twenty-first century.

Fitting schemes of work on multimodal texts into the KS3 English planning cycle

Feedback from English teachers about the schemes of work that are currently part of the proposed KS3 English curriculum model suggests that the study of a whole multimodal text is powerful in terms of helping the pupils' progression of key literary skills. The study of such texts has helped build the confidence of the pupils and this engagement means that they are more likely to transfer these skills to other parts of the English curriculum. These schemes of work, like all of the others, are regularly reviewed as part of the KS3 English planning cycle and the moment they are deemed not fit for purpose they will be amended or omitted. Even though I am passionate about including schemes of work dedicated to the teaching of whole multimodal texts, there is absolutely no point in keeping them as part of the proposed KS3 English curriculum model if they are not helping pupils build on those crucial skills of speaking and listening, reading and writing.

Currently, there are two schemes of work that are dedicated to the study of entire multimodal texts in this proposed KS3 English curriculum. The overarching theme *Multimodal Madness!* takes place at the end of the summer term (summer 2) over the course of five weeks in Year 8 and follows on for a further four weeks at the beginning of the autumn term (autumn 1) in Year 9. This is because the level of empathy and maturity required for the short films that are studied as part of the scheme of work in summer 2 is more suited to those pupils who are about to embark on their final year of KS3 English.

The Year 8 scheme of work *Lights, Camera, Reading and Writing!* is part one of the two schemes of work that comes under the umbrella of the theme *Multimodal Madness!* Table 8.1 shows the first page of the medium-term plan for *Lights, Camera, Reading and Writing!* and it is built on the following Success Criteria which can be found at the bottom of Table 8.1. Pupils will achieve success in this unit if they are able to:

- **Identify** and **label** different camera angles in a sequence of shots from a short film (**Low Level Skills**).
- **Predict** the genre of a short film after closely analysing its opening sequence (**Mid-Level Skills**).
- **Appraise** two or more short films and **decide** which is the most successful in terms of telling a story and **justify** the reasons why (**High-Level Skills**).

The above **Success Criteria** outlines how this first unit is designed to familiarise the pupils with the language of film that can be transferred to the study of other multimodal texts. Being able to transfer the skills of speaking and listening, reading and writing to other curriculum areas is also reinforced across both multimodal units in Years 8 and 9 as it is with any other scheme of work in the proposed KS3 English curriculum model.

Table 8.1 Medium-term plan – lights, camera, reading and writing.

Summer 2 Medium-Term Plan: **Year 8: _Multimodal Madness!_ Part 1**	
Unit Name: _Lights, Camera, Reading and Writing!_	**Duration:** 5 Weeks (_Multimodal Madness!_ Part 2 takes place for 4 weeks at the beginning of Year 9 during Autumn 1)
Learning Cycle 5. Assessing 1: Knowledge 2. Skills — 1. KWHL — 2. Different Text Types — 3. Independent Learning — 4. Feedback	**Overview of unit (National Curriculum Subject Content):** In terms of **(NC)** 'Spoken Language' the pupils will be expected to work **(NC)** _collaboratively with their peers to discuss reading_ of multimodal texts. Pupils will respond to texts that are **(NC)** _Wide, varied and challenging_ and **(NC)** _all pupils read easily, fluently and with good understanding._ Additionally, pupils will also be **(NC)** _learning new vocabulary_ that becomes increasingly challenging over the unit as they **(NC)** _develop an appreciation and love of reading_ multimodal texts. Pupils will not only be encouraged to **(NC)** _read critically through_ [the] _text structure and organisational features_ of multimodal texts and how these present _meaning._ They will also be expected to study **(NC)** _setting, plot and characterisation and the effects of these_ on their intended audiences. Pupils will show knowledge of the **(NC)** _purpose, audience for and context of_ the multimodal texts studied and draw **(NC)** _on this knowledge to support comprehension._ **(NC)** _Pupils will be taught to write accurately, fluently, effectively_ in the _summarising and organising_ of material that may either chart the progress of a multimodal text through narrative accompanying their storyboards or in **(NC)** _well-structured formal expository_ such as film reviews. Pupils can also use the multimodal texts as a stimulus for **(NC)** _stories, scripts, poetry and other imaginative writing._
1. **KWH**L (What do I **k**now? What do I **w**ant to know? **H**ow will I learn?)	*How confident am I with the language of film? *What genres of films do I like and why? *Can I talk about the way a film is structured? *Do I know about the different character types used in film? *How will I transfer my knowledge of film to other areas of the English curriculum?
2. **Different Text Types**	Multimodal instructional texts as well as diagrams that will help pupils understand 'the language of film' (E.G. Mise-en-scene; camera angles, lighting etc); film stills; film reviews; role-play; a selection of short films that can be accessed on the VLE.
3. **Independent Learning**	To work through the skills in the success criteria using a range of independent learning strategies including: Annotation of film stills; storyboarding; filming short films in groups/descriptive writing/film reviews.
4. **Feedback**	Pupils can create their own multimodal texts to feedback their ideas to the class or use speaking and listening as the medium for feedback. E.g. organising a Socratic discussion to question the director's ideas and motives in a film.

Table 8.1 (Continued).

5. **Assessing Knowledge and Skills**	A range of reading and writing questions on the multi-modal texts are differentiated with the relevant media embedded and available on the VLE.
6. KWHL (What have I learned during this unit?)	Response to stage one of the learning cycle; response to success criteria; create a summary/poster/poem about *what I have learned during this unit.*
Success Criteria	
• To **identify** and **label** different camera angles in a sequence of shots from a short film (**Low Level Skills**) • To **predict** the genre of a short film after closely analysing its opening sequence (**Mid-Level Skill**) • To **appraise** two or more short films and **decide** which is the most successful in terms of telling a story and **justify** the reasons why (**High-Level Skills**)	

Nevertheless, even though these schemes of work are innovative and exciting and support the pupils in the development of their speaking and listening, reading and writing skills, the term 'multimodal' is not specifically referred to as a text type that must be studied in the KS3 English curriculum. To work around this fact, I have had to closely examine the ambiguities in the wording of the KS3 English programmes of study so that both schemes of works fulfil the statutory requirements. All of the medium-term plans that can be found in each scheme of work in the proposed KS3 English curriculum model have an area dedicated to the **Overview of unit (National Curriculum Subject Content)**. Both of the *Multimodal Madness! s*chemes of work in Years 8 and 9 are no exception and Figure 8.1 provides a closer look at the **Overview of unit (National Curriculum Subject Content)** on the medium-term plan for the Year 8 scheme of work, *Lights, Camera, Reading and Writing.*

Figure 8.1 clearly demonstrates the large number of the descriptors in the KS3 English programmes of study that are covered within this particular scheme of work. For example, 'pupils will also be **(NC)** *learning new vocabulary* that becomes increasingly challenging over the unit'. The '*new vocabulary*' that the pupils will be learning during this unit includes: mise-en-scène, diegetic sound, non-diegetic sound and three-point lighting. They will also be introduced to the three levels of camerawork used in multimodal texts: shot type, camera angle and camera movement.

As the success criteria states on Table 8.1, the level to which this vocabulary will be understood and used by the pupils is differentiated. However, all pupils are expected to use at least two or three of the new terms that they have learned to help in the understanding of why the directors or 'authors' (DFE: July 2014) make certain choices in their multimodal text. Once two or three of these new words are understood and clearly identified by the pupils in a

97

sequence of shots, they are then encouraged to link these cinematic choices made by the directors or 'authors' to the intended effects on their audience.

The reason I have focused on 'authors' is because this is the most ambiguous word employed in the current KS3 English programmes of study. As the subject content for reading focuses primarily on 'English literature, both pre-1914 and contemporary including prose, poetry or drama' as well as 'Shakespeare (two plays)' and 'seminal world literature' (DFE: July 2014), it means that the statutory requirement to study 'at least two authors in depth each year' is synonymous with the study of 'high-quality' (DFE: July 2014) works of actual literary writers, such as Charles Dickens, George Orwell and Jane Austen. As my degree is in English literature, I think it is wonderful that teachers are encouraged to introduce pupils to their rich literary heritage. However, in this twenty-first century digital age, English teachers also need the pupils to access the 'authors' of texts that they intrinsically understand. If an author is a person who brings something into existence, then why can't the study of a short film fulfil one part of the requirement to study 'at least two authors in depth each year'? Studying one or two short films in detail, I think, is as powerful as studying any one novel, poem or play.

According to their level of ability, Year 8 pupils are expected to read and respond to at least one short film in the *Lights, Camera, Reading and Writing* scheme of work. Figure 8.1 demonstrates that as part of this response to multimodal texts:

> Pupils will not only be encouraged to **(NC)** read critically through [the] text
> structure and organisational features of multimodal texts and how these pre-

---

Overview of unit (National Curriculum Subject Content)

In terms of **(NC)** 'Spoken Language' the pupils will be expected to work **(NC)** *collaboratively with their peers to discuss reading* of multimodal texts. Pupils will respond to texts that are **(NC)** *Wide, varied and challenging* and **(NC)** *all pupils read easily, fluently and with good understanding.* Additionally, pupils will also be **(NC)** *learning new vocabulary* that becomes increasingly challenging over the unit as they **(NC)** *develop an appreciation and love of reading* multimodal texts. Pupils will not only be encouraged to **(NC)** *read critically through* [the] *text structure and organisational features* of multimodal texts and how these present *meaning.* They will also be expected to study **(NC)** *setting, plot and characterisation and the effects of these* on their intended audiences. Pupils will show knowledge of the **(NC)** *purpose, audience for and context of* the multimodal texts studied and draw **(NC)** *on this knowledge to support comprehension.* **(NC)** *Pupils will be taught to write accurately, fluently, effectively* in the *summarising and organising* of material that may either chart the progress of a multimodal text through narrative accompanying their storyboards or in **(NC)** *well-structured formal expository* such as film reviews. Pupils can also use the multimodal texts as a stimulus for **(NC)** *stories, scripts, poetry and other imaginative writing.*

Figure 8.1

*sent meaning. They will also be expected to study **(NC)** setting, plot and char-*
acterisation and the effects of these on their intended audiences.

Therefore, the study of text structure, setting, plot and characterisation is taught through a medium that is familiar to all pupils who are fully immersed in this digital age. For example, storyboarding no longer becomes an arbitrary follow-up task as the pupils are focusing on structure and deciding why the directors or 'authors' have chosen to organise either an opening sequence or an entire short film in a certain way. These reading skills can then be transferred to the analysis of the structure and organisation of a written text.

Another example of how the study of short films helps aid the pupils in their understanding of why the writers of the literary canon or 'high-quality works' (DFE: July 2014) are effective storytellers is by introducing the term 'diegesis' through the close study of diegetic and non-diegetic sound in multimodal texts. More able pupils will be able to recognise these two different levels of narration in the short films and practise applying this higher level of analysis to other written texts.

The creative writing element of the Year 8 *Lights, Camera, Reading and Writing!* unit is referred to in stage five of the learning cycle, *Assessing Knowledge and Skills* (See Table 8.1), which outlines how:

A range of reading and writing questions on the multimodal texts are
differentiated with the relevant media embedded and available on the Virtual
Learning Environment

In my experience, pupils respond positively to the creative writing tasks that are set alongside the embedded extracts from the multimodal texts found on the school's Virtual Learning Environment (VLE). In particular, reluctant writers often enjoy the writing element of the unit as they are given the independence to watch certain clips from the film as many times as they like before they have to type up their responses.

This does require some forward planning by the teacher in terms of booking rooms with computers or accessing laptop trolleys and this is why the VLE reading and writing tasks are clearly highlighted on stage five of the unit's learning cycle; the teacher clearly knows what the pupils are working towards and should organise their planning accordingly. Increasingly, with the advent of smartphones and tablets, pupils can access the work independently from the school as long as they are able to log on to its VLE. Once again, this has proved popular with the majority of pupils who I have taught and many have decided to develop their creative writing outside the school environment.

At the beginning of Year 9, pupils are asked to revise and consolidate their knowledge of this difficult vocabulary introduced at the end of Year 8 through the analysis of non-fiction texts, such as TV adverts.

Table 8.2 shows the first page of the medium-term plan for the Year 9 scheme of work, *Advertisers and their audiences*. After the summer break, the first level in the success criteria is:

- To **revise** different camera angles, mise-en-scene, lighting and soundtrack used in multimodal texts (**Low Level Skills**).

Once the key terminology has been revised and consolidated, it is built upon through the close analysis of non-fiction multimodal texts. Print media is also used as a contrasting text type throughout the unit. In this Year 9 scheme of work, pupils are once again encouraged, through their reading of the multimodal TV adverts and adverts found in magazines, to discuss and evaluate the authors' intended effects on their target audience. Less able pupils are encouraged to master their understanding of the term 'mise-en-scène' and how the use of colour is symbolic in eliciting the desired response from the target audience.

Consequently, when a teacher focuses on a writer's use of colour in a story, play or poem, they can discuss in depth the various connotations associated with those colours as the pupils are encouraged to transfer these visual skills. More able pupils are not only expected to understand and apply the range of complex vocabulary that they have learned over the course of Years 8 and 9 when comparing and contrasting a multimodal TV advert with a magazine advert., but they will also be expected to:

write accurately, fluently, effectively and at length when summarising and organising material, and supporting ideas and arguments with any necessary factual detail.

(DFE: July 2014)

This is also referred to in the **Overview of unit (National Curriculum Subject Content)** in Table 8.2 to show that the statutory requirements for writing are clearly addressed in this scheme of work. In *Advertisers and Their Audiences*, the Year 9 pupils work towards writing either a comparative essay (for more able pupils) or a close analysis of a TV advert (for less able pupils). All of the work covered under the theme *Multimodal Madness!* culminates in stage five of the learning cycle, *Assessing Knowledge and Skills* (See Table 8.2) in this Year 9 scheme of work; specific guidance about the differentiated written assessments is provided in the unit's accompanying sequence of learning.

Table 8.2 Medium-term plan - Advertisers and their audience.

Autumn 1 Medium-Term Plan: **Year 9: _Multimodal Madness_! Part 2**	
Unit Name: _Advertisers and their audiences_	**Duration:** 4 Weeks (_Multimodal Madness_! Part 1 takes place for 5 weeks at the end of Year 8 during Summer 2)
Learning Cycle 5. Assessing 1: Knowledge 2. Skills 1. KWHL 4. Feedback 2. Different Text Types 3. Independent Learning	**Overview of unit (National Curriculum Subject Content):** In terms of **(NC)** 'Spoken Language' the pupils will be expected to work **(NC)** _collaboratively with their peers to discuss reading_ of multimodal texts _across the curriculum_. All pupils will **(NC)** _read easily, fluently and with good understanding_. Additionally, pupils will also be encouraged to continue to have an **(NC)** _appreciation and love of reading_ multimodal texts. Pupils will not only be encouraged to **(NC)** _read critically through_ [the] _text structure and organisational features_ of multimodal texts and how these present _meaning_. They will also be expected to study **(NC)** _setting…and characterisation and the effects of these_ on their intended audiences. Pupils will show knowledge of the **(NC)** _purpose, audience for and context of_ the multimodal texts studied and draw **(NC)** _on this knowledge to support comprehension_ **(NC)** as well as **(NC)** _making critical comparisons across_ a range of print media and multimodal texts. Pupils **(NC)** _will be taught to write accurately, fluently, effectively and at length_ when _summarising and organising material, and supporting ideas and arguments with any necessary factual detail._ Pupils will be taught to draw on their knowledge of **(NC)** _rhetorical devices from their reading and listening to enhance the impact of their writing._
1. **KWH**L (What do I **k**now? What do I **w**ant to know? **H**ow will I learn?)	*How well do I understand the term multimodal texts? *Am I able to transfer my knowledge of how to read a multimodal text to other written texts when reading for meaning? *How confident am I with the terminology associated with multimodal texts and print media? *Do I understand how marketing companies employ a range of persuasive techniques in their campaigns to ensure that the desired target audience will buy their product?
2. **Different Text Types**	Multimodal instructional texts as well as diagrams that will help pupils understand 'the language of film' (E.G. Mise-en-scene; camera angles, lighting etc); film stills; film reviews; role-play; a selection of short films that can be accessed on the VLE.
3. **Independent Learning**	To work through the skills in the success criteria using a range of independent learning strategies including: Annotation of print media and TV advert stills; storyboarding; writing scripts.
4. **Feedback**	Pupils can create their own multimodal texts to feedback their ideas to the class either by producing their own TV advert or by hot seating the TV advert's director. Or, the pupils may use speaking and listening as the medium for feedback. E.g. Through Socratic discussion which will help them verbalise their ideas ready for writing an essay.

Table 8.2 (Continued).

5. **Assessing Knowledge and Skills**	Comparative Essay; Close analysis of a multi-modal text (See *Sequence of Learning* for details of tasks)
6. KWHL (What have I learned during this unit?)	Response to stage one of the learning cycle; response to success criteria; create a summary/poster/poem about *what I have learned during this unit.*
Success Criteria	

- To **revise** different camera angles, mise-en-scene, lighting and soundtrack used in multimodal texts (**Low Level Skills**)
- To **compare** and **contrast** two TV adverts aimed at different target audiences (**Mid-Level Skills**)
- To **evaluate** which is the most effective of the TV adverts in terms of how successful they are in appealing to their target audience and **explain** why (**High-Level Skills**)

The success of both of these multimodal Year 8 and Year 9 schemes of work relies on the teacher's ability to continually refer to the transference of the reading and writing skills covered in the *Multimodal Madness!* units to other parts of the KS3 English curriculum. Even though I firmly believe that the exclusive teaching of multimodal texts in a KS3 English curriculum model, such as the one that I am proposing, is a powerful way of helping the pupils actively engage with reading and writing in a medium that most of them are familiar with, departmental feedback in the KS3 English planning cycle regarding the success of *Multimodal Madness!* is the most decisive factor as to whether the units will remain or not.

As we enter the third KS3 English planning cycle, I am pleased to report that both *Lights, Camera, Reading and Writing* and *Advertisers and Their Audiences* will remain and evolve like the digital technology they both employ. This is because the department believes that whilst they continue to support other areas of the KS3 English curriculum, the *Multimodal Madness!* schemes of work have an important place on the KS3 long term plan and should continue to be taught.

Using multimodal texts to support reading and writing in other KS3 English schemes of work

In the majority of the schemes of work taught across the proposed KS3 English model, multimodal texts are referred to in stage two of the learning cycle on the corresponding medium term plans. Figure 8.2 looks closely at stage two of the learning cycle for the Year 9 autumn 1 and 2 unit, *Why War?*

This example from *Why War?* (a unit which, throughout this book, has been referred to as an example of what a scheme of work looks like from the long-term plan through to the sequence of learning) is typical of how a member of the department is encouraged to start thinking about the different multimodal texts that could be used in their own short-term planning for the teaching of this particular unit, alongside all of the other text types that are outlined in stage two of the medium-term plan's learning cycle.

As always, specific multimodal texts are referred to in the 'Suggested Resources to help fulfil the Week's Learning Objectives' column on the scheme of work's sequence of learning; alternatively, teachers might begin to consider other multimodal texts which suit the ability of their class when they see the medium-term plan. At this stage, teachers are considering extracts from multimodal texts such as documentaries and films, that could be used to consolidate the pupils' understanding of the themes and different contexts that are explored in the unit; ultimately, the multimodal texts chosen by the teacher, whether they are in the sequence of learning or not, must help the pupils work towards the success criteria on the medium-term plan.

Close reading of an extract from a film or documentary also means that pupils are given a wider range of text types that will help them develop their close reading skills. In *Why War?*, pupils read war literature alongside the extracts from multimodal texts to secure their understanding of the unit and to help them become more independent and active readers. The term 'Guided Reading' has long been recognised as a pedagogical framework that supports pupils to become independent readers. Irene C. Fountas and Gay Su Pinnell's, 1996 seminal book, *Guided Reading: Good First Teaching for All Children*,[3] demonstrates how teachers can structure and deliver a successful guided reading programme in the primary phase. According to Fountas and Pinnell (1996, p. 2):

> *The ultimate goal in guided reading is to help children learn how to use independent reading strategies successfully.*

The pedagogy that lies behind Fountas and Pinnell's approach to guided reading also heavily influenced the 'Secondary National Strategy for English'[4] in the mid to late noughties. At this point I have to say that out of the many publications produced, bound and sent to already overcrowded bookshelves in secondary English departments during that time, the guidance and training on guided reading is possibly the only strategy that has fused itself to the way I presently teach. It is also something that is embedded in the KS3 curriculum that I am proposing and all English teachers, including non-specialists, part-time and newly qualified, are encouraged to use the guided reading pedagogy in their teaching.

In addition to the 'guided group reading'[5] referred to in the 'Key Pedagogical Approaches' in the 2008 National Strategy for English publication, Teach-

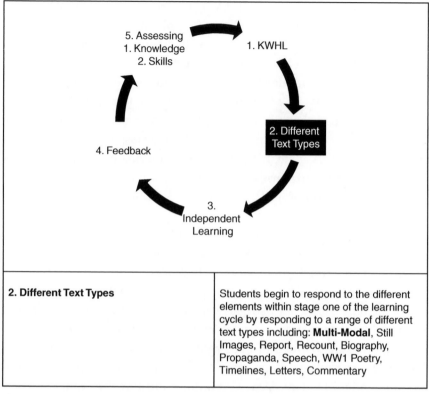

2. Different Text Types	Students begin to respond to the different elements within stage one of the learning cycle by responding to a range of different text types including: **Multi-Modal**, Still Images, Report, Recount, Biography, Propaganda, Speech, WW1 Poetry, Timelines, Letters, Commentary

Figure 8.2 Stage two of the learning cycle.

ing for progression: Reading, a whole section is also dedicated to 'Reading for meaning: understanding and responding to print, electronic and multimodal texts' (DCSF: 2008). Although the vast numbers of strategies prescribed in this area of this publication are difficult to absorb, especially for those teachers who are non-specialists, at least Teaching for progression: Reading recognises the importance of using multimodal texts as way of encouraging guided and consequently independent reading.

Using multimodal texts as a medium through which pupils are encouraged to become independent readers in this proposed KS3 English curriculum is incorporated into the department's guided reading programme. This is when the teacher issues a set of differentiated, colour-coded cue cards to the pupils, depending on their ability and who they are working with, so that they can begin asking relevant generic questions about a text. It is hoped that by KS4, the pupils who are familiar with this visual guided reading programme will be able to recollect at least four or five of these generic questions without being prompted so that they are used to independently questioning a multimodal or written text.

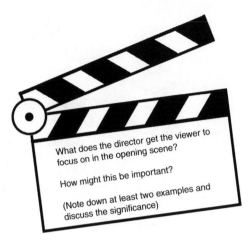

Figure 8.3 Cue card for reading mulitmodal text.

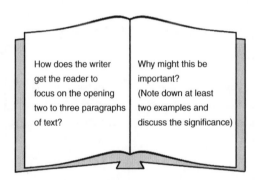

Figure 8.4 Corresponding cue card prompting pupil to question opening text.

Figure 8.3 shows an example of a cue card that is issued to the pupils when reading a multimodal text. This particular cue card poses a series of questions about the opening scene to a multimodal text. Therefore, even though the cue cards are already colour coded, the questions become progressively more difficult so the teacher needs to differentiate even further and tell the pupils how many of the questions they are expected to respond to. Figure 8.4 shows the corresponding cue card used to help the pupils question the opening to a written text. Aside from a slight change in wording to accompany the differing text types, as well as the different visual cues of a director's clipboard in Figure 8.3 and a book in Figure 8.4, if the pupils are trained to use these cards from an early stage in Year 7 by the end of Year 9 they will be able to transfer these reading skills across multimodal and written texts.

Figures 8.5 and 8.6 provide further examples of corresponding guided reading cue cards. Once more, they clearly demonstrate how pupils are asked to

Figure 8.5 Cue card for reading mulitmodal text.

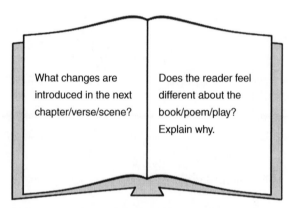

Figure 8.6 Corresponding cue card prompting pupil to question opening text.

question multimodal and written texts in the same way. The emphasis on this guided reading programme is to encourage the pupils to no longer compartmentalise their knowledge, but instead transfer these crucial reading skills not simply across different text types, but also across the rest of the KS3 curriculum. By training the pupils into this way of thinking from an early stage in their KS3 English curriculum, there will be less need to firefight at KS4, as these reading skills are already subliminally embedded into their consciousness. All of the medium-term plans make reference to the guided reading cue cards in the 'Support' and 'Challenge' sections to remind teachers how they can be used in their lessons, as well as introducing new staff, non-specialists and long-term supply staff to a programme that anyone can deliver and differentiate in their own lessons.

This chapter ends where it begins. Media and film contribute a great deal of money to the British economy. Film studios in the UK alone attract huge investment and it seems incomprehensible that the term 'multimodal texts' is missing from the current KS3 English programmes of study. In the same way that the quality of the written texts used in the proposed KS3 English curriculum model are appraised during the planning cycle, the validity of using specific multimodal texts is also continually reviewed. However, at the beginning of the twenty-first century, I would never advocate omitting multimodal texts from a KS3 English curriculum model, especially the teaching of whole multimodal texts. In my career so far, the power of reading and writing through the stimuli of moving images and sound is such that I know the written responses that I will get from all of the pupils will be of a very good to high standard simply because of the inclusive nature of multimodal texts.

Notes

1 *Statutory guidance: National curriculum in England: English programmes of study*, Department for Education, September 2013 (updated, July 2014); https://www.gov.uk/government/publications/national-curriculum-in-england-english-programmes-of-study.

2 *Digital Natives, Digital Immigrants*, Prensky, M., 2001; http://www.marcprensky.com/writing/Prensky%20-%20Digital%20Natives,%20Digital%20Immigrants%20-%20Part1.pdf.

3 Fountas, I. C. and Pinnell, G.S., 1996. *Guided Reading: Good First Teaching for All*. New Hampshire: Heinemann, p. 2.

4 *Secondary Framework for English*, Department for Children, Schools and Families, archived in 2011; http://webarchive.nationalarchives.gov.uk/20110113104120/http://nationalstrategies.standards.dcsf.gov.uk/secondary/secondaryframeworks/englishframework.

5 *Teaching for progression: Reading*, Department for Children, Schools and Families, December 2008; http://webarchive.nationalarchives.gov.uk/20110113104120/http://nationalstrategies.standards.dcsf.gov.uk/node/153786.

CHAPTER 9

Key Stage 3 English homework

The debate surrounding homework is a hotly contested one and is often described as the elephant in the room, as there are two opposing opinions stretched across a very thin pedagogical line. At one end of the continuum are the teachers, who believe that homework is vital in helping support a pupil to consolidate their learning outside of school hours. However, at the other end of the continuum line, there are teachers who believe that homework serves no purpose and is burdensome for the pupils.

There is also a belief that homework contributes to a teacher's already over-crowded workload, as it can generate a great deal of marking, in addition to its being deemed yet another administrative task – classroom teachers often have to follow up and deliver sanctions during their break and lunchtime, as they use this time to discuss with pupils the reasons behind their failure to meet the homework deadline. The numerous teaching blogs and online forums in the UK are testament to the thousands of opinions that fuel each side of the homework debate. Having read through many of these blogs and forums over the years it is difficult to ascertain if there is or ever will be an overriding winner of this highly contentious issue.

In the 'Findings from the survey' from the *Key Stage 3: The wasted years*[1] report, there is a whole section dedicated to the finding that 'The quality of homework in Key Stage 3 is too variable and does not effectively enable pupils to consolidate or extend their learning' (Ofsted: 2015). This negative subtitle is substantiated with the following claims from senior leaders. The first is the startling revelation that 'One headteacher acknowledged that, sometimes, teachers just set homework for the sake of it', whilst 'A small number of senior leaders questioned the value and impact of homework in Key Stage 3' (Ofsted: 2015). Although these candid responses from some senior leaders are astonishing, it is the feedback from the pupil questionnaires with regards to homework that is even more disconcerting for KS3 English teachers:

Pupils' responses to the online questionnaire gave further evidence that, too often, homework is not helping them to consolidate or extend their learning. Approximately half of the Key Stage 3 pupils said that their homework either never, or only some of the time, helped them to make progress. They felt that sometimes it was given for the sake of it, was not useful and not linked to the learning in the lesson.

(Ofsted: 2015)

Whatever side of the debate a teacher may find themselves on, if a school has a homework policy that has to be adhered to, then the homework that they set must help the pupils 'consolidate or extend their learning'; otherwise, it is a pointless exercise for all involved.

Over the past ten years, it has become increasingly easy for KS3 English teachers to download individual lesson plans, resources and homework tasks from the Internet. Although these resources, such as the homework tasks, can be useful, if they do not add to the holistic approach to a KS3 English curriculum model at any level of planning then they simply become arbitrary tasks that are being set for the sake of it. Equally, in Ofsted's 2009 report, *English at the crossroads*, inspectors observed that:

In secondary schools, too much homework was confined to simple revision or completing written work begun in class.[2]

KS3 English departments need to take care that they don't simply see homework as an extension of what they started in class unless the outcome is intrinsically linked to moving the pupils' learning forward.

In Chapter 6, 'LAC and SPAG: Divisive or Cohesive Abbreviations in the KS3 English Curriculum?', there is reference made to the weekly spelling tests to be set as part of the SPAG lessons in Year 7. However, these tests in which the pupils have one week to practise the spellings for homework are not simply put into this proposed KS3 English curriculum model for the sake of setting SPAG homework. As has been clearly outlined in Chapter 6, this purposeful weekly revision of the Year 3 to 4 and Year 5 to 6 spelling lists[3] (or spelling lists A and B as they are referred to in this proposed KS3 English curriculum model) are to make sure that all Year 7 pupils, no matter which primary school they have come from, are secondary ready and have mastered the statutory spelling lists.

Homework in this proposed KS3 English model

Suggested homework in a sequence of learning

The 'Suggested Homework' column in a scheme of work's sequence of learning is 'Suggested' and not mandatory. In the same way as the preceding 'Suggested Resources to help fulfil the Week's Learning Objectives' column does not simply dictate what resources should be used during that particular week, the 'Suggested Homework' column is also there to provide a range of differentiated ideas that may be useful in helping the classroom teacher set purposeful homework for their pupils.

Similar to the thinking behind the suggested resources column, it is assumed that the class teacher who is solely responsible for planning their lessons in the short term understands their pupils better than the person designing and implementing the KS3 English curriculum model; therefore, it is up to the classroom teacher to decide whether they will set homework or not during that week. If they choose to set homework, as they feel it will aid the pupil's learning, the classroom teacher has the final say as to what the tasks might be. Ultimately, the 'Suggested Homework' column is to demonstrate the types of activities that pupils could undertake outside of school to help them reach the next stage of learning in the scheme of work.

Table 9.1 is an example of how the 'Suggested Homework' column is linked back to the week's mandatory learning objectives in the Year 8, spring 2 scheme of work, *Read All About It!*. This particular scheme of work falls under the overarching KS3 English theme, 'Writing in the style of' (in spring 2 of Year 7, pupils write 'in the style of' an action and adventure writer and in Year 9, the pupils write 'in the style of' a travel writer). In Read All About It! the Year 8 pupils are expected to write 'in the style' of a tabloid and broadsheet journalist and this week two excerpt from the scheme of work in Table 9.1 shows a range of proposed differentiated homework tasks that could potentially support the pupils in their understanding of the different types of print journalism. Content from the 'Suggested Resources to help fulfil the Week's Learning Objectives' column has been deliberate omitted in Table 9.1 to demonstrate how the suggested homework is differentiated and directly correlates back to the mandatory learning objectives for week two.

The 'Learning Objectives' in Tables 9.1 and 9.2 are representative of the mandatory requirements of any sequence of learning in this proposed KS3 English curriculum model. The skills outlined in these learning objectives are differentiated so that all pupils have the best chance to demonstrate mastery in their learning by the end of that week. Equally, the suggested resources and home-

Table 9.1 Spring 2: Sequence of learning: Year 8: Writing in the style of…Read all about it!

Week	Learning Objectives	Suggested Resources to help fulfil the Week's Learning Objectives	Suggested Homework
2.	1. To **label** the features of the front pages of a tabloid and a broadsheet newspaper (**Low-Level Skill**) 2. To **compare** and **contrast** the front pages of a tabloid and a broadsheet newspaper (**Mid-Level Skill**) 3. To **re-create** a tabloid front page in the style of a broadsheet front page (**High-Level Skill**)		Bring in an example of the front page of a tabloid and/or a broadsheet newspaper. **Challenge** Find out the definitions of the following terms: Headline; Masthead; Strapline; Lead Article (**Further Challenge:** Put them into a sentence to show an understanding of the meaning of the term) **Challenge** Annotate and explain the editor's decisions behind the chosen: headline, masthead, strapline and lead article on the front page of a tabloid or/and a broadsheet.

Table 9.2 Autumn 2: Sequence of learning: Year 7: The cauldron of characterisation: Will the real Scrooge please stand up?

Week	Learning Objectives	Suggested Resources to help fulfil the Week's Learning Objectives	Suggested Homework
2.	1. To **label** different images with a range of adjectives (**Low-Level Skill**) 2. To **construct** a cauldron of characterisation based on inferences made about a character in the opening stages to a text (**Mid-Level Skill**) 3. To **explain** the meanings behind a number of clichés to a twenty-first century audience (**High-Level Skill**)		Complete a colour-coded synonym wheel using the words: bad, sad, angry, lonely, mean and jealous at its epicentre. **Challenge** To complete a character profile of Scrooge (**Support:** Provide a template for those pupils who need explicit guidance) **Challenge** To write the opening three paragraphs to an imaginary book aimed at a twenty-first century reader (aged between 11 and 14) called, *Don't be a Scrooge!*

work columns presented in the sequence of learning are often differentiated to remind the teacher that not everybody in their classroom will be able to complete the same work at the same rate of learning, especially if they are undertaking the task in their own time.

In Ofsted's *Key Stage 3: The wasted years?* report, it is claimed that 'in four of the schools, pupils said that everyone got the same homework, regardless of their ability' (Ofsted: 2015). Differentiated tasks are vital when setting homework in KS3 English, because if the pupils are to complete these tasks in an environment outside of the classroom, then they need to have every chance of success; otherwise, the whole process is demoralising. For example, to help the pupils achieve the first of the 'Learning Objectives' in Table 9.1 which is, '*To **label** the features of the front pages of a tabloid and a broadsheet newspaper*', then asking the pupils to bring in an example of one or both types of newspaper means that they are already researching the similarities and differences between the two types of press, because they have to find out what they are before they can acquire the necessary research. Not only is this a relatively straightforward task, it is also purposeful.

Likewise, the first of the 'Learning Objectives' in Table 9.1 is a low-level skill to provide the foundations to the week's learning as it is, '*To **label** different images with a range of adjectives*'. The corresponding homework in the 'Suggested Homework' column in Table 9.1 is to '*Complete a colour-coded synonym wheel using the words: bad, sad, angry, lonely, mean and jealous at its epicentre*' which is a straightforward and creative task that will support the pupil's learning and help them achieve this first learning objective in week two of the Year 7 sequence of learning for 'Will the real Scrooge please stand up?'. As the use of colour-coded synonym wheels are part of the suggested 'Writer's Toolkit' starter activities in the Year 7 SPAG lessons, this homework task could be set during the SPAG lesson as opposed to the weekly spelling test if the teacher feels that it is of more intrinsic value to their pupils' learning during that week.

Equally, both Tables 9.1 and 9.2 demonstrate a range of increasingly more difficult homework tasks that not only builds on the pupil's learning, but also challenges them too. By giving pupils the option to undertake a range of more rigorous homework tasks of their choice, it means that they will have the best chance of mastering the higher level learning objectives in a sequence of learning. In order to fulfil these higher level 'Learning Objectives', such as '*To **re-create** a tabloid front page in the style of a broadsheet front page*' in Table 9.1 and '*To **explain** the meanings behind a number of clichés to a twenty-first century audience*' in Table 9.2, the pupils will have to start from the lower level learning objectives and build their skills and knowledge throughout the week, which includes completing a range of tasks in the 'Suggested Homework' column. By undertaking more rigorous KS3 English homework tasks, it means that the pupils have the best chance of mastering the skills needed to succeed with the higher level learning objectives.

As these are all 'Suggested Homework' tasks, the classroom teacher has the autonomy to decide what is the best course of action for the KS3 English pupils in front of them whilst also adhering to their school's homework policy. As with any resources, it is hoped that collaborative feedback informs colleagues of homework tasks that have either worked or are to be steered cleared of. Ultimately, this feedback during and at the end of the planning cycle means that successful homework tasks can be added to the existing scheme of work as it continues to evolve. Another benefit of providing explicit tasks in the 'Suggested Homework' column, is that it supports non-English specialist teachers, long-term supply teachers or those who are newly qualified and need guidance and direction in setting purposeful, differentiated homework in this proposed KS3 English curriculum model.

Homework projects

If the controversial topic about homework is fiercely debated, then the notion of homework projects being implemented into any potential KS3 English curriculum model is even more contentious. Yet again, there are lots of pros and cons as to why homework projects should be used in KS3. However, as with the arguments outlined above in terms of setting weekly homework on a sequence of learning, the success of a homework project is closely tied with its purpose and as to whether it supports a pupil in their learning. Other logistical implications of homework projects include how well they fit in with the whole-school homework policy. In the same way as downloading sheets of work or resources from a website can prove to be an arbitrary exercise if not carefully planned into a lesson, homework projects that don't form an important part of a holistic KS3 English curriculum can add no intrinsic value to a pupil's learning. Due to the length of homework projects, decisions as to where and when they should be implemented in a KS3 English curriculum model need to be discussed at the end of each planning cycle as they form a major part of any scheme of work.

However, it is vital that KS3 English pupils are given opportunities to be autonomous learners and as such homework projects that are carefully planned and successfully embedded into a scheme of work mean that the pupils are able to experience real-life skills such as research and time management. In the Ofsted report, *English at the crossroads*, it was reported:

> *As they got older, pupils were given fewer rather than more opportunities to work independently or to exercise choice. Preparation for GCSE examinations exacerbated this by focusing on what teachers and students described as 'spoon-feeding'.*

(Ofsted: 2009)

KS3 English curriculum models that embrace carefully planned homework projects will not simply support a pupil's development of the key skills of speaking and listening, reading and writing; they will also help the pupil recognise their own capabilities and this can serve to build their resilience and confidence. These are life skills which are crucial to success at GCSE if English teachers are to avoid 'spoon-feeding' and firefighting in the summer term of Year 11 in KS4.

A homework project forms part of one scheme of work per year group in this KS3 English curriculum model that I am proposing. There is a homework project researching William Blake in Year 7 and a group homework project based on the issues surrounding homelessness in Year 9. The Year 8 homework project in Figure 9.1 is embedded into the autumn 1 spoken language scheme of work, *What's my voice?*, which consolidates the pupils' knowledge about the nature of formal and informal language as well as examining the similarities and differences between spoken and written texts. Logistically, in terms of marking, these homework projects have to happen at different points in the academic year to avoid a deluge of projects being handed in at the same time, awaiting to be assessed. Therefore, in this proposed KS3 English curriculum model, the Year 8 English homework project is completed in the second half of the autumn term; the Year 7 English homework project is completed towards Easter and the Year 9 English homework project is to be arranged as a speaking and listening presentation at the beginning of the summer term.

The homework project outlined in Figure 9.1, *My Language Autobiography*, not only builds on the pupils' prior learning; each section provides them with a range of tasks that they can choose from to help them secure their learning about spoken language. *My Language Autobiography* is set at the beginning of the scheme of work and pupils are given a set date in which it is to be handed in. Depending on the ability of the group and how many sections the class teacher wants completed, pupils usually have around six weeks in which to hand in their final project.

The sections within the project are very broad in their scope and it may be that, for differentiation purposes, the class teacher wishes their group to focus on one or two sections and support them even further by setting smaller and

Section One:

In this section, I am going to write about the importance of English as a world language.

Section Two:

In this section, I am going to explain the **origins** of my name and surname. I am also going to share what I learned whilst researching **names.**

Section Three:

In this section, I am going to talk about **learning to talk**. I am going to ask my family about how, when and what I said when I first began to talk.

Section Four:

In this section, I am going to create a language survey and ask different people how they talk and write in different situations and talk about the different results that I have found and why I think they are interesting. I will talk about anything that that has surprised me in my survey findings.

Section Five:

In this section, you are going to look at how speaking to your **friends** has affected your accent and dialect. Has your variety of English been influenced by contact with other accents and dialects? If so, where? Give examples.

Figure 9.1 Year 8 English: My language autobiography: homework project.

more manageable tasks within each section. Likewise, a teacher might want to use one of the sections as a homework focus for each week. For example, the teacher may want to model a variety of survey types to help the pupils decide how they will go about collating and evaluating their primary research for section four of the homework project. Once the teacher has decided what the class

Table 9.3 My language autobiography: homework feedback sheet.

Year 8: My Language Autobiography: *Homework Feedback Sheet*		
Section	**Task**	**Assessment**
One	The importance of English as a world language.	Strength:
		Strength:
		Target:
Two	Researching **names** and their **origins**.	Strength:
		Strength:
		Target:
Three	**Learning to talk**.	Strength:
		Strength:
		Target:
Four	**Language Survey** and **Findings**	Strength:
		Strength:
		Target:
Five	**Accents** and **Dialects**	Strength:
		Strength:
		Target:

outcomes will be from *My Language Autobiography*, then it is up to the pupils to work independently on putting their projects together.

It is important that a homework project such as *My Language Autobiography* becomes a sustainable part of any robust KS3 English curriculum model; hence it is important that it is evaluated biannually or annually as part of a departmental review. Table 9.3 came about at the end of the planning cycle between 2014 and 2015 because, although the Year 8 pupils were thoroughly engaged with the project in the first year of this proposed KS3 English curriculum model, it was difficult to assess and get the projects back to the pupils in a time frame that meant the pupils were not waiting too long for their feedback. The pro forma in Table 9.3 can also be differentiated like the homework project itself. The class teacher might want to focus on one or two as opposed to all five of the headings, so that the formative assessment provided is meaningful and helps move the pupil's learning on to the next stage according to their ability. During the planning cycle from 2016 to 2017, pupils will also be encouraged to upload their projects digitally to the school's Virtual Learning Environment (VLE). In an age of smartphones and tablets, it means that a teacher can check on the pupil's homework project at any time and provide almost instantaneous feedback, which will help avoid the monsoon of marking at the end of the six-week time frame allocated.

Notes

1 *Key Stage 3: The wasted years?*, Ofsted, September 2015; https://www.gov.uk/government/publications/key-stage-3-the-wasted-years.

2 *English at the crossroads: An evaluation of English in primary and secondary schools, 2005/08*, Ofsted, June 2009; http://webarchive.nationalarchives.gov.uk/20131216215503/http://www.ofsted.gov.uk/news/english-crossroads-0.

3 *Statutory guidance: National curriculum in England: English programmes of study*, Department for Education, September 2013 (updated, July 2014); https://www.gov.uk/government/publications/national-curriculum-in-england-english-programmes-of-study.

CHAPTER 10

Key Stage 3 English: Where next?

Whilst researching this book I have looked at a number of documents produced by various governments and Ofsted as I felt it was important to highlight (a) the consistencies in educational policy at national level and (b) the inconsistencies in educational policy at national level over the past fifty years. The seminal 2013 Ofsted report, *Moving English forward*,[1] is one of the documents that I have frequently referred to throughout this book because it spearheaded the KS3 English working party that I became a part of; this group of amazing teachers re-energised my belief and passion that a robust and evolving KS3 English curriculum is vital if pupils are to succeed in their GCSE English language and English literature exams at the end of KS4.

According to *Moving English forward*, one of the main features of an outstanding English curriculum model is that it 'is continuously reviewed and improved in light of national developments' (Ofsted: 2013). It has been my aim in this book to take this outstanding feature one stage further by suggesting that the KS3 English curriculum 'is continuously reviewed' not only in light of national developments, but more importantly in light of departmental developments.

The next planning cycle

At the beginning of this third KS3 English planning cycle, I am already thinking ahead to what the beginning of the fourth KS3 English planning cycle may look like. Recurring questions such as: Will there be different levels of staffing in the department? Will we need an extra KS3 speaking and listening assessment in Year 8? Will the 2017–2018 cohort of Year 9s be as able as those who have just started Year 7? Such questions are already infiltrating the next planning cycle, because for this proposed KS3 English curriculum model to be outstanding, it has to absorb departmental changes and evolve accordingly.

The fact that the planning cycle in this proposed KS3 English curriculum model allows the department to reflect termly through online surveys and discussion, as well as allocating designated time at the end of the year to modify long- and medium-term plans and sequences of learning accordingly, means that it is better prepared to respond to any great shifts in educational policy on a national level. This KS3 English curriculum model that I am proposing has already evolved during a turbulent time in education; policy at national level has been thrust upon schools in England rapidly over the past five years. Yet, this proposed KS3 English curriculum model has evolved alongside these changes because it is reviewed regularly and relies on the collaboration of all the teachers in the department.

The *Key Stage 3: The wasted years?*[2] report was published at the same time as the second planning cycle in this proposed KS3 English model commenced. One year later, at the beginning of the third planning cycle, there is a confidence within the English department of it working towards and already fulfilling the recommendations made in the report. This is due to the fact that even though the report was a landmark in raising awareness of the importance of KS3 at a national level, the department had already been working relentlessly to make sure that Years 7 to 9 are prepared for KS4 English before *KS3: The wasted years?* was published.

I felt a sense of vindication when the September 2015 report was published, as the importance of KS3 English and raising its profile has been something that I have been passionate about since the early stages of my career. For this to be finally acknowledged in a dedicated Ofsted report that solely focused on the importance of KS3 in England meant that the ensuing and long-overdue debate in schools and in the media was warmly welcomed.

A checklist for success

As Ofsted's earlier *Moving English forward* report was extremely influential in the construction of this proposed KS3 English curriculum model and the working party that delivered the two countywide conferences in 2014 and 2015, it is important to measure any success against the following statement made in the report:

> *Secondary schools should also ensure that the English curriculum at Key Stage 3 has a clear and distinct purpose that is explained to students and builds in, where possible, tasks, audiences and purposes that engage students with the world beyond the classroom.*

(Ofsted: 2013)

It has been one of my aims during this book to demonstrate how the KS3 English curriculum model that I am proposing strives to make sure that pupils in Years 7, 8 and 9 are excited to come to an English lesson, but more importantly, leave that lesson and want to transport their knowledge and skills to not only different areas of the curriculum, but also to other parts of their everyday lives.

The subsequent recommendation for secondary schools in the *Moving English forward* report to 'strengthen whole-school literacy work across all departments to ensure that students extend and consolidate their literacy skills in all appropriate contexts' (Ofsted: 2013) is a work in progress and I am excited to see how this contributes to the future development of this proposed KS3 English curriculum model as it continues to evolve.

Another checklist in the *Moving English forward* report that this proposed KS3 English curriculum model is successfully working towards includes:

- Innovation and creativity.
- All staff work very well together because there is a strong shared purpose and commitment to the same goals.
- Provision for pupils is reviewed collaboratively and good practice is shared routinely and effectively.
- All members of the team, including newly qualified teachers, have good opportunities to contribute to developments. (Ofsted: 2013)

One area of the checklist in the *Moving English forward* report that needs to be developed during this and proceeding KS3 English planning cycles is that of student voice. There needs to be more documented evidence of 'the response of pupils, to review the impact of work across reading, writing and speaking and listening' (Ofsted: 2013). Over the past two and a half years, the evaluation process has relied heavily on the responses and the collaboration of the department. During this time, pupils have informally told their English teachers what they enjoy and what they think needs improving in their KS3 English lessons; however, a more formalised way of documenting this pupil feedback is needed so that it can become an official part of the KS3 English planning cycle.

The future of KS3 English at national level

In ten years' time, there may not even be such a thing as a KS3 English curriculum in schools across England. Currently, England, Northern Ireland and Wales have a National Curriculum that is split into discrete key stages across the primary and secondary phase. However, for one part of the United Kingdom, that is about to change. In two years' time, a new National Curriculum will be available to schools in Wales; by September 2021, this curriculum will be in place and the concept of Key Stages will have been scrapped. According to the Welsh government website:

> *This new approach was informed by Professor Graham Donaldson's independent review of curriculum and assessment arrangements in Wales, **Successful Futures ...** in February 2015 which provided the foundations for a twenty-first century curriculum shaped by the very latest national and international thinking.[3]*

By the time that the new National Curriculum for Wales will have been implemented in 2021, there will have also been a general election across the United Kingdom. Often a change in government also means a national shift in educational policy. Teachers are excellent at accommodating and working with these major national vicissitudes even though they prove to be extremely stressful because of the sheer volume and rapid nature of the changes.

At the time of writing, the current government is also floating the idea of letting new grammar schools open across England for the first time in eighteen years, as it believes it is conducive to promoting the idea of social mobility. There are so many questions, ambiguities and uncertainties surrounding the future of secondary education in England that to commit to any type of KS3 curriculum English model may seem like a ludicrous idea. However, it is the planning cycle, rather than the curriculum model itself, that is the most important factor for English departments across England to consider.

The KS3 English planning cycle outlined in Chapter 2 underpins the way in which this proposed KS3 English curriculum model is managed. This book, like the planning cycle, has come full circle. As the next planning cycle begins it is absolutely crucial to make sure that the central premise outlined in Chapter 1, that any KS3 English curriculum model is robust and remains relevant through collaboration, evaluation and re-construction, continues.

I firmly believe if there were any further radical changes to the curriculum on a national level, such as Key Stages ceasing to exist in England as they have done in Wales, then a successfully embedded planning cycle will help an English department accommodate any further changes to a National Curriculum for pupils aged between 11 and 14 because of its cyclical nature. The ongoing process of review-plan-evaluate-implement-review has meant that this KS3 English model that I am proposing has gone from strength to strength. Due to the success of the planning cycle outlined in Chapter 2, I have a passionate belief and confidence that it is able to withstand and work alongside any further overhaul in the secondary English curriculum at national level in the future.

Notes

1   *Moving English forward: Action to raise standards in English*, Ofsted, April 2013; https://www.gov.uk/government/publications/moving-english-forward.
2   *Key Stage 3: The wasted years?* Ofsted, September 2015; https://www.gov.uk/government/publications/key-stage-3-the-wasted-years.
3   *Curriculum Reform*, Welsh Government, 2016; http://gov.wales/topics/educationandskills/schoolshome/curriculum-for-wales-curriculum-for-life/?lang=en.

Index